Anti-Inflammatory Diet for

20-Day Meal Plan and Delicious Recipes for Everyone

© **Copyright 2021 - All rights reserved.**

This document is geared towards providing exact and reliable information in regard to the topic and issue covered.

- From a Declaration of Principles which was accepted and approved equally by a Committee of the American Bar Association and a Committee of Publishers and Associations.

In no way is it legal to reproduce, duplicate, or transmit any part of this document in either electronic means or in printed format. All rights reserved.

The information provided herein is stated to be truthful and consistent, in that any liability, in terms of inattention or otherwise, by any usage or abuse of any policies, processes, or directions contained within is the solitary and utter responsibility of the recipient reader. Under no circumstances will any legal responsibility or blame be held against the publisher for any reparation, damages, or monetary loss due to the information herein, either directly or indirectly.

Respective authors own all copyrights not held by the publisher.

The information herein is offered for informational purposes solely and is universal as so. The presentation of the information is without contract or any type of guarantee assurance.

The trademarks that are used are without any consent, and the publication of the trademark is without permission or backing by the trademark owner. All trademarks and brands within this book are for clarifying purposes only and are owned by the owners themselves, not affiliated with this document.

Table of Contents

INTRODUCTION 5
CHAPTER 1. THE ANTI-INFLAMMATORY DIET 7
CHAPTER 2. THE CAUSES OF INFLAMMATION 15
CHAPTER 3. WHO THE DIET IS AIMED AT? 17
CHAPTER 4. WHAT IT PROVIDES AND ITS BENEFITS 19
CHAPTER 5. LISTS OF ANTI-INFLAMMATORY FOODS 23
CHAPTER 6. 20-DAY MEAL PLAN 29
CHAPTER 7. BREAKFAST 31
CHAPTER 8. LUNCH 48
CHAPTER 9. DINNER 66
CHAPTER 10. SNACKS 82
CONCLUSION 100

INTRODUCTION

Anti-inflammatory diets are very popular right now because many people have inflammation due to their immune systems attacking the body and causing damage. Inflammation can lead to illnesses such as arthritis, fibromyalgia, and even Alzheimer's disease. The anti-inflammatory diet for beginners is a great plan for those looking to feel better, live longer, and get relief from their chronic disease symptoms.

The goal of an anti-inflammatory diet is to eat foods that combat inflammation in your body. These foods are filled with antioxidants that will heal your cells and balance any excess hormones. These are great for people that have systemic inflammation. People with joint, skin, or bone issues may also benefit from this type of diet.

A pro-inflammatory diet has a higher amount of unhealthy foods like sugar and animal products that promote inflammation in the body. An anti-inflammatory diet is made up of healthier foods like fruits, vegetables, and fish. Stored fat is also considered an inflammatory agent so it is best to avoid traditional fats like butter and oils.

People could respond differently to different diets so it is important to consider your intolerance level when choosing which diet will work best for you. There are plenty of anti-inflammatory diets available but the ones to be explored here are the Mediterranean, macrobiotic, and Ayurvedic diets.

Anti-inflammatory diets have a lot to offer for people that are suffering from chronic inflammation. This type of diet is not for weight loss although it can help you with your weight loss goals if you include healthy fats in your diet. These diets can be costly if they incorporate exotic foods so you might need to adjust them to fit your budget and make them work within your lifestyle.

The best way to find out which one works for you is to try them out for yourself and then see how you feel after a couple of weeks on each one.

How much should I eat?

It is essential to note that anti-inflammatory diets require a lot more food than a "normal" diet does. Your meals need to be big and there aren't any snacks in this program. This is crucial because if your body is not getting enough fuel it will start using its fat supply as an energy source instead of burning fat from the foods you are eating. This can lead to very unhealthy weight gain if you don't adjust your diet to reflect this fact. Eating too much will also make it difficult for your body to store fat because there isn't any room for it, so many people end up with excess water weight which doesn't do anything positive for the body.

What foods are safe?

There is a huge variety of foods in the anti-inflammatory diet that have very beneficial effects on your body. Eating natural, organic fruits and vegetables is important because they are filled with antioxidants and nutrients that can help you heal from inflammation. Lean meats like chicken, turkey breast, and fish can be included in meals to give your body a good source of Protein: if you are following the plan for weight loss. Poultry has been shown to help reduce joint pain while fish offers benefits for eye health. Non-starchy vegetables such as leafy greens like kale, Swiss chard, spinach, and collard greens also have beneficial effects on health and should be eaten daily. Whole grains like brown rice, quinoa, and wheat berries can be great for weight loss because they are high in fiber and complex carbs.

There are also some vegetables and fruits with natural anti-inflammatory properties, such as:

Ginger: Ginger has been used for centuries by Asian communities as a natural cure for all sorts of health issues. Studies have shown that this root can help with arthritic pain. It should not replace traditional medications but it is very beneficial to add to your diet if you experience pain from inflammation. Ginger tea, ginger cookies, or any other culinary creation easily adds ginger to your daily dietary intake.

Garlic: garlic is another culinary staple for good reason. Studies have shown that those persons who eat garlic have a lower risk of heart disease, lower cholesterol, and are less likely to develop cancer cells. It is especially good for skin health since it is known to control acne and eliminate all signs of inflammation in the body. The best way to enjoy garlic would be in a gourmet meal or simply sautéed with olive oil as part of your vegetable intake.

Lemon juice: lemon juice has been used as a natural cleanser and disinfectant for years because of its antibacterial properties. It can also help cure respiratory problems such as coughing by adding healing properties to the mucus membranes. This is most beneficial for people with chronic respiratory issues. Adding lemon juice to a meal can help your body absorb all of the nutrients from your food.

Monkfish: monkfish is a type of fish that is consumed in Southeast Asian cultures. It has been shown to reduce joint pain and inflammation and also helps eliminate cancerous cells. The oil in monkfish helps reduce inflammation by preventing the body from breaking down healthy tissue and replacing it with dead tissue.

CHAPTER 1. THE ANTI-INFLAMMATORY DIET

The anti-inflammatory diet is a set of guidelines that you can apply to what you eat. In general, a diet filled with a wide range of plant-based foods, whole grains, lean proteins, and good fats will decrease inflammation but also prevent any future flare-ups.

The adverse effects of eating a standard American diet have repeatedly been proven by scientists (Walker, 2015). Heavily processed and packaged foods often contain sugar, sodium, and unhealthy fats, which are inflammation-promoting ingredients. Besides the high amount of refined carbohydrates, the average American eats daily.

Conversely, an anti-inflammatory diet focuses on eating wholesome, unprocessed foods that are high in antioxidants, and other nutrients that maintain good health.

Some noteworthy benefits of following an anti-inflammatory diet, getting active, and sleeping more, include:

- A decrease in symptoms of autoimmune disorders such as arthritis, IBS, and lupus
- Reduction of inflammatory markers
- Improved blood sugar levels, and better cholesterol and triglyceride levels
- Higher energy levels
- Stable mood

THE BASIC GUIDELINE OF ANTI-INFLAMMATORY DIET

The focus is on a well-balanced diet filled with a variety of vegetables and fruit. These low-calorie foods promote digestion, help manage weight, and keep inflammation in check, which prevents cellular damage. Brightly colored fruits and vegetables are particularly healthy as they contain more phytochemicals—plant compounds are known to reduce inflammation

Whole grains are preferred over refined grains. Oats, quinoa, barley, chia, and sorghum are good examples of unrefined grains high in fiber, antioxidants, and other nutrients that are beneficial to your health. Whole grains promote a healthy immune response in the body by providing valuable nourishment to beneficial gut bacteria. Other high-fiber foods like beans and fermented foods like kefir, kimchi, and pickles, balance gut bacteria and fight inflammation and disease.

When it comes to fats, the anti-inflammatory diet recommends using plant-based options like olive oil instead of trans fats and saturated fats from animal products. Olive oil has proven health benefits.

Furthermore, increasing your intake of omega-3 fats is highly advocated. This healthy fat directly reduces inflammation. Fish and walnuts are good omega-3 sources. Most other nuts and seeds also contain healthy fats, as well as Protein: and other valuable micronutrients, to boost your immune response.

Consuming red meat is limited while on the anti-inflammatory diet as it contains high amounts of undesirable fats, sodium, and antibiotics and hormones, which increases inflammation. When red meat is eaten, cooking methods such as grilling should be avoided as the blacked parts of meat can lead to inflammation. Overall, fish and poultry are better choices of animal protein.

Green tea and red wine are two powerful beverages often consumed on anti-inflammatory diets due to their high antioxidant properties. You're also allowed to drink coffee.

3 KEY ASPECT OF ANTI-INFLAMMATORY DIET

That covers the basics of an anti-inflammatory diet, but there are three aspects I want to discuss in more detail.

Free Radicals and Antioxidants

I just going to come out and say it: the American diet is toxic. It's high in saturated fat, hidden sugars, sugar alcohols, preservatives, etc. which increases the formation of free radicals. Now, free radicals are necessary to kill invading bacteria, but when they're in excess, they will cause cell damage through a process called oxidation.

When you cut an apple in half and leave it on your desk, it will turn brown in a matter of minutes—this is oxidation, and it happens in our bodies. Free radicals play an integral part in the oxidation process. These atoms are volatile, and when they come in contact with ordinary atoms, they steal electrons to make up for what they're missing. This starts a chain reaction, and more and more free radicals are created, and cells are damaged (oxidation).

An increase in bad cholesterol is one of the many negative impacts free radicals and subsequent oxidation have on our health.

Besides an unhealthy diet, we are also exposed to external environmental toxins that spark a free radical increase. Carbon monoxide, ultraviolet rays, pesticides, and radiation exposure from technology are some external ecological toxins.

Luckily our bodies have evolved natural antioxidant nutrients to help fight off these free radicals. The only problem is when following the standard American diet, and the external factors, our bodies can't handle all the free radicals. It is then up to us to take extra antioxidants to help out a little. Antioxidants can provide free radicals with the missing electron they're searching for, thereby neutralizing them.

Omega-3 and Omega-6

The standard American diet, with its high levels of trans and saturated fat and omega-6 fat, stimulates inflammation in the body.

On the flip side, unsaturated fats (polyunsaturated and monounsaturated) calm inflammation and decrease the risk of heart disease. Soybean, sunflower, corn oil, and other vegetable oils contain a mix of mono- and polyunsaturated fats in various amounts, and are neutral—they do not affect heart health. The main problem with omega-3 and omega-6 is the ratio. A healthy ratio is 1/1, but in America, you can expect anything from 1/10 to 1/20. Since Omega-6 is pro-inflammatory, you can see why this is very problematic. If you don't eat food with enough omega-3 fatty acids or drink a supplement, the imbalance will cause your body to suffer.

Omega-3 isn't as available far and wide as in the days before the Industrial Revolution. Before mass food production became the norm, the soil was nutrient-rich, and produce wasn't treated with preservatives to keep it fresh during the long journey to the store—it was locally grown and organic. Cattle also had free access to omega-3 fat while grazing around. Today the picture looks much different; the soil is depleted, pesticides and preservatives are part of the process, and cattle are stuck in feedlots where they are injected with hormones and antibiotics. All these natural sources of omega-3 fatty acids are destroyed, and we're limited to finding it only in fish, vegetables, and supplementation.

If we don't get enough omega-3 in our diet, we will experience the following:

- Acne
- Arthritis
- Depression
- Allergies
- Asthma
- Inflammatory bowel syndrome
- Hypertension
- Heart disease
- Cancer
- Diabetes

Common Sensitive Foods

People react to food differently. The good thing about the anti-inflammatory diet is you can customize the menu to suit you. Follow the diet for 30 days, and if you still struggle with inflammation, you can go through a process of elimination. Use a food journal to track what you're eating and how you feel afterward, and if a particular food is not causing you discomfort, add it back into your diet.

Some common triggers include:
- Nightshades (tomatoes, goji berries, eggplant, bell peppers, potatoes, etc.)
- Gluten (barley, rye, oats, etc.)
- Eggs
- Soy (tempeh, soy sauce, miso, etc.)
- Shellfish and fish
- Wheat
- Dairy
- Nuts

TYPES OF ANTI-INFLAMMATORY DIETS

There are different types of diet for anti-inflammatory:

- The Mediterranean diet
- The DASH diets
- The vegan or vegetarian diet
- Whole food diet
- Plant-based diet

The Mediterranean diet is by far the most extensively researched anti-inflammatory diet. With the DASH diet coming in a close second.

The various ingredients of any anti-inflammatory diet work to reduce inflammation and lead to positive effects on your well-being. The Mediterranean diet and other anti-inflammatory ways of eating emphasize the lifestyle aspects that you need to change for the best results.

If it all sounds a little overwhelming, make one change at a time. This way you're more likely to make it a lifestyle and not just a diet. Finding a balance between addressing stress healthily, spending time with your family, exercising, and sleeping enough is equally important as the food choices you make.

CHAPTER 2. THE CAUSES OF INFLAMMATION

Inflammation is an immune response that prepares your body to fight against foreign invaders like bacteria or viruses. It does so by attacking them with enzymes, proteins, or cells that are active in an inflammatory process referred to as acute inflammation. The most common cause of this type of inflammation are infections such as colds, flu, and others. Smoking also causes acute inflammatory processes because it leads to oxidative stress.

When inflammation occurs repeatedly it can cause the following conditions:

1. Chronic Inflammation – It's a worsening of the inflammatory response that goes beyond what is normal to a chronic state. It's also known as Systemic Inflammation (the whole body). Common symptoms of this are recurring colds or flu, sinus infections, or bronchitis.

2. Acute Inflammation - This is a normal inflammatory response that is triggered when you have an infection, cut yourself, get injured, etc., and is controlled by the same cells that fight off foreign bodies and infections.

3. Auto-Inflammation – It's a phenomenon in which inflammation occurs even without any triggers or tissues of the body. It is a normal phenomenon in the body's immune system but could also be triggered by substances such as alcohol, sugar, etc.

4. Allergic reactions (also referred to as hypersensitivity) - these are a direct result of an overreaction of the immune system when it detects an antigen or particles that trigger an inflammatory response. This can lead to symptoms ranging from pain, swelling, and hives to full-blown allergies and asthma attacks. Some foods and drugs may cause allergic reactions in some people for unknown reasons.

5. Post-Infectious Syndrome - This occurs when an illness that causes inflammation leads to a chronic state of inflammation. An example of this is arthritis after strep throat. This is usually temporary but, in some cases, can be present for months or years, especially when the person does not get proper treatment and changes their lifestyle.

6. Cell Injury and Ischemia - Inflammation is also known as an acute reaction to cell injury which may be caused by excessive amounts of free radicals in the body, clogged arteries, or high blood pressure. The inflammatory process includes redness, pain, and swelling due to capillary dilatation and vasodilation (dilation or contraction of blood vessels).

7. Metabolic Syndrome - This is a common condition that includes high blood pressure (hypertension), increased cholesterol levels, high triglyceride levels, increased body weight or obesity, and diabetes.

8. Heart Disease: Atherosclerosis - This is when fatty deposits build up inside the arteries which can eventually cause heart attacks or strokes. It occurs when LDL cholesterol (low-density lipoProtein: cholesterol) is deposited in the walls of the arteries instead of being removed by the liver as it should. Although oxidation of LDL cholesterol happens in normal physiology, too much LDL cholesterol can be dangerous to your blood vessels and heart.

9. Hepatitis - This is a liver inflammation caused by viral or bacterial infections.

10. Auto-Immune Diseases - Some people have an autoimmune disease that causes the immune system to attack healthy tissue such as joints, muscles, skin, eyes, and ovaries. These diseases are associated with an overreactive immune system (in which a certain part of the immune system mistakenly attacks its tissue).

11. Tumor Necrosis Factor-Induced Inflammation - this is a phenomenon that occurs when there is excessive production of "Tumor Necrosis Factor" (TNF). TNF is a Protein: that is present in the cells of many tissues in the body. It plays a crucial role in the inflammatory process to defend the tissues. However, overproduction of TNF can cause an excessive inflammatory response which causes cell death and tissue damage.

12. Vascular Inflammation - Inflammatory reactions that occur on or around the vessel walls (capillaries) are considered vascular inflammation. This type of inflammation is more common when there is an infection near blood vessels, such as meningitis or pneumonia.

13. Respiratory Inflammation – It occurs when the lungs are inflamed or infected. This can occur in several ways:

a. Allergic reactions to dust or pollution (for example, asthma)

b. Infection of the airways by bacteria/fungus in the upper respiratory tract

c. Foreign body obstruction (for example, foreign body inhalation).

CHAPTER 3. WHO THE DIET IS AIMED AT?

Chronic inflammation is a result of a persistent immune response that can cause significant damage to our tissues. Inflammation is an essential component of our immune system, as it helps to remove dead cells and pathogens as well as regulating healing. The problem arises when our bodies experience harmless triggers that have no impact on our health. In other words, we may experience symptoms of inflammation without actually being in danger or at risk for injury or illness.

This diet helps control chronic inflammatory responses by consuming foods that reduce the amount of pro-inflammatory cytokines in the body and promoting those that have potent anti-inflammatory properties. It is as simple as eating a diet that is based on whole, natural foods and avoiding inflammatory foods such as highly processed meats and dairy.

The conventional way to deal with inflammation is through the use of drugs. While these medications can help reduce inflammation, the side effects can be devastating and they may not work as effectively as we like. Individuals who have tried these types of medications while living a generally healthy lifestyle, then begin to realize that there is an alternative way to address their symptoms. The same approach can be implemented by anyone for less than half the cost of many prescription drugs! The least expensive form of treatment is simply eating real foods that are in general accepted as good for us.

If we look at the body as a machine that needs to be kept in good working order, then we should be doing all we can to provide the body with the tools it needs to stay healthy. A healthy diet is one such tool. We already know this. But how are drugs more effective than simply eating well and avoiding inflammatory triggers, especially when drugs are much more expensive? The answer lies in a kind of double-whammy effect on the immune system: anti-inflammatory medications tend to dampen one part of the immune system, while inflammation itself tends to activate another part of the immune system (the so-called "adaptive" or "acquired" immune component).

One such example of how a chronic inflammatory response can be triggered by a "healthy" food is provided in my own life. At one point, I tried to eat whole grains and gluten-free foods to avoid inflammation. I ended up consuming more pro-inflammatory foods than I realized and the inflammation came back worse than ever. This made me realized the value of avoiding highly inflammatory foods such as processed meats while eating other healthy foods.

What makes some foods turn pro-inflammatory is not known, but it is clear that the immune system responds differently depending on the food. This is because there are different receptors for particular groups of foods, such as our "taste" receptors. These receptors send signals to our brain to tell us how something tastes, and they also send signals to our immune system. It appears that many of these taste centers in the brain have an impact on the development or severity of inflammatory disorders we develop later in life.

One of the reasons a diet that promotes anti-inflammatory foods is so effective is because the foods provide many different nutrients that target inflammation. Some examples include:

– Omega-3 fatty acids (found in fish and fish oil)

– Vitamin C (found in citrus, berries, broccoli, and tomatoes)

– Various flavonoids (found in fruits and vegetables)

– Magnesium is found in many green leafy vegetables, nuts, beans, and seeds. This mineral has potent anti-inflammatory properties. It also helps to prevent blood clotting, reduce blood pressure and heart disease risk.

– Phenolic compounds found in vegetables such as artichokes, garlic, and cauliflower

How does this diet help to reduce inflammation? Although the details are not yet clear, the consensus seems to be that certain foods contain bioactive substances that promote inflammation. Another important factor is that certain foods may stimulate immune cells to release inflammatory triggers such as cytokines. Since these compounds are not stored in the body like antibodies, they cause a non-specific or generalized response, which means they can create a series of reactions throughout our tissues. Some evidence suggests that this response may be triggered by food allergies.

The anti-inflammatory diet provides a range of nutrients that are beneficial to our health. Making foods that contain these substances even richer in the diet is a good way to support the body's natural response to inflammation. This approach makes sense from a biological perspective, but also an economical perspective. We can achieve the same results as most medications by eating food!

CHAPTER 4. WHAT IT PROVIDES AND ITS BENEFITS

Many people who choose this diet want to reduce inflammation throughout the body to prevent or try to reduce the amount of pain they have in their body, especially in their joints. But there are some other health benefits that you may be able to get when you go on this diet plan, and some of them may even surprise you!

THE HEALTH OF YOUR HEART WILL IMPROVE

Having the strongest and healthiest heart possible is essential for those who want to live a long and healthy life. Following an anti-inflammatory diet is a great way to proceed whenever you want to lower the risk of heart disease while lowering your blood pressure and bad cholesterol levels.

All these factors will work together to ensure your heart stays healthy and can make you feel much better. Although it is not always necessarily the leading cause of any heart disease, the American Heart Association has stated that patients with heart disease are often more likely than other patients to have high inflammation in the body. This means that it is possible that having higher levels of inflammation could lead to higher risks for the heart. Lowering that inflammation and making sure you have it under control, can help protect your heart.

There have been some researches done to try and find out if there is a relationship between high levels of C-reactive proteins and heart disease. CRP is a Protein: that is released into the bloodstream and signals the onset of inflammation. According to the clinic that conducted this research, CRP could be as predictive as the cholesterol to use as the risk of heart disease. When you get on an anti-inflammatory diet, you will be able to eat more fiber, which can reduce CRP levels along with the risk of heart disease.

In 2002, the study was published in the New England Journal of Medicine following a Harvard study. In this study, CRP was found to be a stronger indicator of cardiac risk in a person than cholesterol. The study measured LDL and CRP in about 28,000 women in America for over eight years. At the end of it, the study recommended that patients should be tested for their CRP levels and their cholesterol levels since both would show different results and could detect heart problems more quickly.

CAN PREVENT DIABETES

Diabetes is a disease that is commonly increasing in our society. It is important to learn how to adopt a healthy lifestyle so that we have a better chance of preventing this disease. Whether you have this disease or not, or whether you have a genetic predisposition to it, eating healthy and adding a little good exercise to your routine can help prevent it.

If you want to prevent diabetes, anti-inflammatory is a great way to start. One of the most important factors in the development of type 2 diabetes is overweight and maintaining this weight for a long time. Extra weight causes a lot of problems, and one of these is inflammation throughout the body. Since the anti-inflammatory diet can reduce the amount of inflammation found in the body, it is the perfect option to help prevent diabetes. Also, the healthy foods you eat can make weight loss easier, which saves you even more.

Since you are reducing unhealthy carbohydrates, processed sugars, and other things that can cause inflammation and type 2 diabetes, you are going to prevent and even reduce the symptoms of type 1 diabetes and type 2 diabetes. Your mood will improve, your risk of diabetes and your symptoms will drop, you will lose weight, and have more energy, and much more!

YOUR BRAIN IS GOING TO START WORKING BETTER

Chronic inflammation has been proved to increase the amount of depression that occurs, and can also contribute to mental exhaustion, anxiety, indecision, and brain fog. When you spend some time eating processed foods, carbohydrates, bad fats, and sugar, you will experience many abnormalities in your blood sugar levels. Over time, you will find that it leads to insulin resistance, and also an increase in body fat and inflammation.

It has been found that taking foods that cause inflammation of the body causes intestinal discharge and dysbiosis. Studies have pointed out that there is a direct link between unhealthy intestine, inflammation, and depression.

Learning to cut off foods that naturally need to be avoided during the anti-inflammatory diet may help you achieve a more careful mental state. Learn to replace some of these empty calories with many phytonutrients in the form of brightly colored vegetables and fruits that can fight inflammation and give an extra boost to your brain.

SEE YOUR SKIN START TO GLOW

Have you ever thought about how what you eat will affect the skin you're in? Your skin is forgotten often, but it's the biggest organ in your body, and it shows what's going on inside you. Your diet can affect all the different parts of your health, and an excellent visual cue on how your health is doing is how your skin looks and feels.

Having chronic amounts of inflammation and skin problems are related to each other. For example, an unbalanced amount of intestinal flora is 37 percent more likely to be linked back to acne problems. Food intolerances (which many of us have no idea we have in the first place), bad fats, sugar, and processed foods alter the intestinal flora as well. If you don't take care of it right away, it could cause intestinal losses, which will naturally increase the amount of inflammation found through the body.

A lot of skin problems are related to nutrition. Problems such as rashes, itching, rosacea, psoriasis, spots, acne, and dullness are all linked by some dietary component behind them. That is why many people who follow the anti-inflammatory diet and learn to cut processed foods, soy, dairy products, gluten, yeast, and refined sugars, find that they are able not only to reduce the amount of inflammation found in the body but that it will help them improve the appearance of their skin.

You're also helping your skin to take all the minerals, vitamins, and antioxidants needed to keep it glowing.

TAKES AWAY THE BLOAT

Dairy products and gluten are causing problems for your digestive health, and you may notice that you experience a lot of gas, constipation, diarrhea, and swelling when you consume some of these products, especially if you have an intolerance to them.

Dysbiosis is the main cause of these symptoms and occurs when all the bad ones begin to overwhelm the good microorganisms in the intestine. It also happens in what is known as SIBO (or excessive intestinal bacterial growth), when the bacteria begin to move to another area of the stomach, usually the small intestine, where they should not be.

The point of having this intestinal flora is to make sure that all the bad stuff stays out of your body, and you don't get sick as often. But if there is any reason why the flora is compromised, then some bacteria that should not be there will settle in the stomach and this will result in some inflammation.

If you find that you need help to speed up the process or are worried about having followed an unhealthy diet for too long and you may need extra work, some prebiotics and probiotics can help you balance your bowels.

Probiotics can be absorbed with supplements, or you can eat a variety of fermented foods, including kimchi, kefir, and sauerkraut, to help those beneficial bacteria found in the body. Then there is prebiotics, and these include options such as jicama, onions, and garlic will be vital because they help provide the nutrients that good bacteria need to stay healthy and strong.

One thing to note, though, is that if you have SIBO, you should not take probiotics or prebiotics. With this condition, you are already addressing the issue of bacteria that grow too fast and end up in an area where they shouldn't. Make sure to talk to your doctor about it.

EASIER TO GET THE CRAVINGS UNDER CONTROL

If you have found that you have a lot of intense cravings regularly, especially for foods that are full of carbohydrates and high sweetness factor, then this is a sign that something is not right with your body, and it is time to work to make it right. Refined sugars, as well as many artificial sweeteners, start a vicious circle of inflammation throughout the body, and the food cravings you have will continue to make things worse because of how the chemicals in your body change, especially those in your brain and intestines.

It's hard to break the craving cycle. But the anti-inflammatory diet can intervene to try to make things a little easier. It can do that by filling you up with a lot of the good things your body needs. You'll be able to remove toxins from your sugars and cleanse your body, ensuring that it's easier to clean up those cravings and not feel them so much in a short time.

According to Dr. Frank Lipman, a functional and integrative medicine physician, sugars are something that we need to avoid as much as possible. Having some in fruit may not be bad, but the extras that come in our foods, or that we seek out in baked goods and more are causing a lot of adverse health effects that we need to focus on.

CHAPTER 5. LISTS OF ANTI-INFLAMMATORY FOODS

MOST POWERFUL ANTI-INFLAMMATORY FOODS

Little or gradual modifications are typically sustainable, more suitable for the body to adjust to, and may decrease your chances of responding to your old habits. Then instead of emptying your locker, including setting out for the Mediterranean, you can start a small step at a point and begin an anti-inflammatory diet.

By appending anti-inflammatory diets that fight inflammation to your diet, you can start to repair your body outwardly, making any sharp differences by regaining health at the cellular level. When you discover foods that heal your body also satisfy your taste buds, you can eliminate the wrong foods that create inflammation without feeling guilty. Let's get a look at 15 of the best anti-inflammatory foods you can combine with your diet.

1. Green Leafy Vegetables

It is the principal food you require to fill your refrigerator when combating inflammation. Fruits and vegetables are wealthy in antioxidants that restore cellular health as well as anti-inflammatory flavonoids. If you have complexity eating green leafy vegetables, you can make anti-inflammatory vegetable juices where you can merge greens.

For instance, when you consume biceps, it is abundant in antioxidant vitamins A plus C and vitamin K, which can defend your brain upon oxidative stress induced by free radical damage. Consuming biceps can also shield you from vitamin K deficiency.

2. Bok Choy (Chinese cabbage)

Bok choy, also known as Chinese cabbage, is an excellent source of antioxidant vitamins and minerals. Recent research shows that bok choy also contains more than 70 antioxidant phenolic substances. These include acids called hydroxycinnamic, which are robust antioxidants that remove free radicals. As a versatile vegetable, bok choy can be used in many dishes outside of Chinese cuisine, so it is one of the best anti-inflammatory foods.

3. Celery

The benefits of celery in recent pharmacological research include antioxidant and anti-inflammatory properties, as well as preventing heart disease, which helps improve blood pressure and cholesterol levels. Celery seeds have impressive health benefits in themselves to reduce inflammation and fight bacterial infections. It is an excellent source of antioxidants and vitamins as well as potassium.

Also, balance is the key to a healthy body without inflammation. An excellent example of inflammation-related mineral balance is celery, the right mix of sodium and potassium-rich foods. Sodium brings liquids and nutrients, while potassium removes toxins. We know that sodium in processed foods is high, but our usual diets are not rich in potassium. Without this pairing, toxins can accumulate in the body and cause inflammation once again. One of the benefits of celery is an excellent source of potassium, as well as antioxidants and vitamins.

4. Beetroot

The most evident marker of food full of antioxidants is its deep color. The umbrella category of antioxidants contains a large number of substances. In general, they fight to repair cell damage caused by inflammation. The beet gives the signature color of antioxidant betalain and is an excellent anti-inflammatory. Among the benefits of beet when added to the diet, we can see that it increases the levels of potassium and magnesium that fight cell repair and inflammation.

When a balanced diet is done, calcium-rich anti-inflammatory foods, as well as magnesium, allow the body to better process what is consumed.

5. Broccoli

It is no mystery that broccoli is a worthy addition to either diet, the perfect vegetable for healthful eating. It is valuable for the anti-inflammatory diet. Broccoli is excellent in both potassium and magnesium, including its antioxidants, which are expressly potent anti-inflammatory factors.

Broccoli holds essential vitamins, flavonoids, and carotenoids and is a significant root of antioxidant power. They go together to decrease oxidative stress inside the body and to inhibit chronic inflammation, including cancer development.

6. Blueberries

In particular, quercetin, which is also found in blueberries, appears as an antioxidant and a powerful anti-inflammatory (the pigments found in some plants). Quercetin, which is found in citrus, olive oil, and dark fruits, is a flavonoid (a useful substance or phytonutrient that is common in fresh foods) that fights inflammation and even cancer. The presence of quercetin is one of the health benefits of blueberries. In a study seeking IBD treatment, noni fruit extract was used to influence intestinal flora and colon damage by inflammatory diseases. Due to the effects of the extract, quercetin produced significant anti-inflammatory effects.

In another study, they found that consuming more blueberries slowed down cognitive decline and improved memory and motor functions. Scientists in this study believed that these results were due to blueberry antioxidants, which prevent the body from oxidative stress and reduce inflammation.

7. Pineapple

Generally, when taken as a supplement, quercetin is coupled with bromelain, a digestive enzyme, which is one of the benefits of pineapple. After years of use as part of an anti-inflammatory food protocol, bromelain is observed to have immune modulation capabilities - i.e., it helps to regulate the immune response that generates unwanted and unnecessary inflammation.

Pineapple also helps to improve heart health because it contains an active bromelain enzyme. Pineapple is nature's answer to those who struggle with blood clotting and take an aspirin a day for those who want to reduce the risk of a heart attack. Bromelain has been found to stop blood platelets from sticking together or accumulating on the walls of blood vessels (known causes of heart attacks or strokes).

The benefits of pineapple, high in addition to other disease-specific antioxidants that help prevent the formation of vitamin C, vitamin B1, potassium, and manganese supply. Pineapple is full of phytonutrients (plant nutrients), which are useful in addition to many medicines to reduce the symptoms of some of the most common diseases we see today.

8. Salmon Fish

Salmon is an outstanding source of indispensable fatty acids, and it is estimated one of the most fabulous omega-3 foods. The omega-3 is the joint active anti-inflammatory agent that demonstrates consistently decreasing inflammation, including reducing the requirement for anti-inflammatory drugs.

The analysis explains that omega-3 fatty acids decrease inflammation as well as reduce the risk of persistent diseases like heart disease, skin cancer, and arthritis. Omega-3 fatty acids remain concentrated inside the brain and are necessary for cognitive and behavioral function.

Between anti-inflammatory foods, fish and meat are essential components. One of the risks of farm fish is that they do not include the same nutrients as naturally fed fish.

9. Bone Water

Bone juices contain minerals in forms that your body can easily absorb; calcium, magnesium, phosphorus, silicon, sulfur, and others. These include chondroitin sulfates and glucosamine. It is used as additional substances to reduce inflammation, arthritis, and joint pain.

When patients suffer from leaking bowel syndrome, they are advised to consume a large number of bone waters containing collagen and amino acid proline and glycine, which may help to improve the damaged cell walls of the leaking intestine and the inflammatory bowel.

10. Walnut

When you follow a diet that does not have a lot of meat, nuts, and seeds, you meet your Protein: and omega-3 needs. To get anti-inflammatory nutrients, you can add omega-3 rich walnuts to green leafy salads with plenty of olive oil, or you can eat a handful of walnuts between meals.

Phytonutrients help prevent metabolic syndrome, cardiovascular problems, and type 2 diabetes. Some plant nutrients in walnuts are not found in other foods.

11. Coconut Oil

Much can be written about how herbs and oils work together to form anti-inflammatory partnerships. Lipids (oils) and spices are strong anti-inflammatory compounds, especially coconut oil and turmeric components. A study in India found that antioxidants in coconut oil reduce high levels of inflammation and improve arthritis more quickly than medical drugs.

Also, oxidative stress and free radicals are the two main causes of osteoporosis. Coconut oil is a leading natural cure for osteoporosis because its benefits include combating such free radicals with high levels of antioxidants.

You can easily use it in the kitchen as well as topical preparations. As heat-resistant oil, it is an excellent choice for sauteed anti-inflammatory vegetables.

12. Chia Seed

Fatty acids found in nature are more balanced in our typical diets than those we usually consume. For example, Chia seeds contain omega-3 and omega-6, which should be consumed with each other.

Chia contains essential fatty acids alpha-linolenic and linoleic acid, mucin, strontium, minerals containing vitamins A, B, E, and D, antioxidants containing sulfur, iron, iodine, magnesium, manganese, niacin, and thiamine.

Chia is a seed that can reverse inflammation, regulate cholesterol, and lower blood pressure, which is incredibly beneficial for heart health. Also, by reversing oxidative stress, one is less likely to develop atherosclerosis while regularly consuming chia seeds.

13. Flax Seed

Flaxseed, an excellent source of omega-3 and phytonutrients, is full of antioxidants. Lignans are unique fiber-related polyphenols that provide antioxidant benefits for anti-aging, hormone balance, and cellular health. Polyphenols promote the growth of probiotics in the intestine and may also help eliminate yeast and Candida Fungus in the body.

Before using flaxseed with your anti-inflammatory foods, grind it in a mill to ensure that your digestive system can easily access the benefits of the seeds.

14. Turmeric

The prime component of turmeric is curcumin, an active anti-inflammatory Ingredient. Turmeric has been confirmed to be invaluable in anti-inflammatory nutrition.

While curcumin is among the significant anti-inflammatory and anti-proliferative agents within the world, aspirin (Bayer, etc.), and ibuprofen (Advil, Motrin, and so on.) have been discovered to have no sound effects.

Because of its noble anti-inflammatory qualities, turmeric is extremely useful in assisting people in treating rheumatoid arthritis (RA). A study from Japan assessed its correlation with interleukin (IL), an inflammatory cytokine identified to be connected in the RA process. It found that lead "significantly decreased these markers of inflammation.

15. Ginger

Used in fresh, dried, or extracts, ginger is another immune modulator that helps reduce inflammation caused by overactive immune responses.

Ayurvedic medicine has revealed that ginger can improve the immune system before the recorded date. Ginger is believed to be effective in increasing your body temperature, helping to disperse toxin accumulation in your organs.

Ginger's health benefits include reducing inflammation in allergic and asthma diseases.

INFLAMMATORY FOODS TO AVOID

When you diet with anti-inflammatory foods, you naturally begin to eliminate pro-inflammatory foods and substances. There is nothing as satisfying as a diet rich in whole foods.

The primary suspects are saturated and trans fatty acids. These fats in processed foods increase inflammation and risk factors for obesity, diabetes, and heart disease.

Omega-6 oils that exceed the balance of omega-3 create inflammation in the body. Unfortunately, the University of Maryland Medical Center says, "A typical diet contains 14-25 times more omega-6 fatty acids than omega-3 fatty acids.

Simple, refined sugars and carbohydrates are more culprits than foods that cause inflammation. Limiting refined foods is an essential factor in an anti-inflammatory diet. All grains can replace refined carbohydrates because whole grains are essential food sources. By using fermented yeasts, you can break down nutrients and gain better access to the body.

Also, establishing a regular physical activity routine can help prevent the occurrence or recurrence of systemic inflammation.

CHAPTER 6. 20-DAY MEAL PLAN

Day	Breakfast	Lunch	Dinner	Snacks
1	Fruity Flaxseed Breakfast Bowl	Balsamic Salmon Spinach Salad	Shrimp and Vegetable Curry	Okra Fries
2	Cinnamon & Coco Milk Muffins With Specially Prepared Sweet Potato	Mediterranean Tuna-Spinach Salad	Vegetable and Chicken Stir Fry	Potato Sticks
3	Perky Paleo Potato & Protein: Powder	Chicken Stir-Fry	Blackened Chicken Breast	Zucchini Chips
4	Pumpkin Puree Porridge	Ground Turkey and Spinach Stir-Fry	Green Hummus	Beet Chips
5	Choco Chia Banana Bowl	Mango Chicken Meal	Parsley 'N Lemon Kidney Beans	Spinach Chips
6	Blueberry Breakfast Blend	Sweet Potato Platter	Moroccan Salad	Sweet & Tangy Seeds Crackers
7	Quick Quinoa With Cinnamon & Chia	Salty Caramel Dip	Pumpkin Soup	Plantain Chips
8	Plum, Pear & Berry-Baked Brown Rice Recipe	Anti-Inflammatory Turmeric Gummies	Healthy Shrimp and "Grits"	Quinoa & Seeds Crackers
9	Good Grains With Cranberries & Cinnamon	Delicious Snow Crab	Creamy Pesto Chicken	Apple Leather
10	Seared Syrupy Sage Pork Patties	Chicken Lettuce Wraps	Gingered Vegetable Curry	Roasted Cashews

11	Waffles Whipped With Perfect Plantain Pair	Chicken Breast with Cherry sauces	Baked Chicken Breast With Lemon & Garlic	Roasted Pumpkin Seeds
12	Turkey With Thyme & Sage Sausage	Black Rice Bowl with Tahini, Pistachios, and Raspberries	Pork Tenderloin With Dijon-Cider Glaze	Spiced Popcorn
13	Sweet and Savory Breakfast Hash	Baked Sweet potatoes	Nutty and Fruity Amaranth	Cucumber Bites
14	-Minute Avocado Toast	Grilled Sauerkraut Avocado Sandwich	Salmon and Dill Pâté	Spinach Fritters
15	Healthy Chickpea Scramble Stuffed Sweet Potatoes	Ground Turkey and Sweet Potato	Nutty and Fruity Garden Salad	No-Bake Strawberry Cheesecake
16	High-Protein: Breakfast Bowl	Zucchini and Ground Turkey	Broccoli-Sesame Stir-Fry	Raw Lime, Avocado & Coconut Pie
17	Green Smoothie Bowl	Popcorn Chicken	Lemony Mussels	Pudding Muffins
18	Fruity Bowl	Spicy Chicken and Cauliflower	Cherries and Quinoa	Black Forest Pudding
19	Quinoa & Pumpkin Porridge	Curried Shrimp and Vegetables	Celery Root Hash Browns	Pineapple Sticks
20	Apple Omelet	Sheet Pan Rosemary Mushrooms	Blueberry Chia Pudding	Fried Pineapple Slices

CHAPTER 7. BREAKFAST

1. FLAXSEED BREAKFAST FRUITY BOWL

Preparation time: 8 minutes

Cooking time: 5 minutes

Servings: 1

Ingredients:

For the Porridge:

- ¼-cup flaxseeds, freshly ground
- ¼-tsp cinnamon, ground
- 1-cup almond or coconut milk
- 1-pc medium banana, mashed
- A pinch of fine-grained sea salt

For the Toppings:

- Blueberries, fresh or defrosted
- Walnuts, chopped raw
- Pure maple syrup (optional)

Directions:

1. In a medium-sized saucepan placed over medium heat, combine all the porridge ingredients. Stir constantly for 5 minutes, or until the porridge thickens and comes to a low boil.
2. Transfer the cooked porridge to a serving bowl. Garnish with the toppings and pour a bit of maple syrup if you want it a little sweeter.

Nutrition: Calories: 780, Fat: 26g, Protein: 39g, Sodium: 270mg, Total Carbs: 117.5g, Dietary Fiber: 20g, Net Carbs: 97.5g

2. CINNAMON & COCO MILK MUFFINS WITH SPECIALLY PREPARED SWEET POTATO

Preparation time: 25 minutes

Cooking time: 35 minutes

Servings: 4

Ingredients:

- Coconut oil for greasing
- 1-pc small sweet potato, roasted
- 3-Tbsps flaxseed, ground, soaked in ½-cup water
- 2-Tbsps olive oil
- ¾-cup coconut milk
- ½-cup pure maple syrup
- 1/8-tsp cloves, ground
- 1/8-tsp nutmeg, ground
- ¼-cup coconut flour
- ½-tsp Himalayan salt
- 1-cup brown rice flour
- 1-Tbsp baking powder
- 1-Tbsp cinnamon, ground
- 1-tsp ginger, ground
- 1-tsp turmeric, ground

Directions:

1. Preheat your oven at 400°F. Meanwhile, grease your muffin tray lightly with coconut oil.
2. By using a wooden skewer, pierce about a dozen holes around the sweet potato. Cook it for an hour, or until soft.
3. Slice the potato crosswise and scoop out its flesh into a large mixing bowl. Pour the soaked flaxseed—combining the specially prepared egg mixed with the potato—olive oil, coconut milk, and maple syrup. Mix well to a smooth consistency.
4. Stir in all of the dry ingredients in another mixing bowl. Mix well until thoroughly combined. Blend the dry and wet mixtures, and mix well until fully incorporated.
5. Fill each section of the muffin tray up to 2/3 full. Put the tray on the oven's middle rack. Bake for 35 minutes, or until the muffins turn golden brown.

Tips:

You can replace ground flaxseeds with ground chia seeds, and, raw or unpasteurized honey for maple syrup.

When preparing the meal ahead, you can freeze the muffins and serve them whenever.

Nutrition: Calories: 510, Fat: 17g, Protein: 25.5g, Sodium: 320mg, Total Carbs: 73.4g, Dietary Fiber: 9.7g, Net Carbs: 63.7g

3. PERKY PALEO POTATO & PROTEIN: POWDER

Preparation time: 8 minutes

Cooking time: 0 minutes

Servings: 1

Ingredients:

- 1-pc small sweet potato, pre-baked and fleshed out
- 1-Tbsp Protein: powder
- 1-pc small banana, sliced
- ¼-cup blueberries
- ¼-cup raspberries
- Choice of toppings: cacao nibs, chia seeds, hemp hearts, favorite nut/seed butter (optional)

Directions:

1. In a small serving bowl, mash the sweet potato using a fork. Add the Protein: powder. Mix well until thoroughly combined.
2. Arrange the banana slices, blueberries, and raspberries on top of the mixture. Garnish with your desired toppings. You can relish this breakfast meal either cold or warm.

Nutrition: Calories: 302, Fat: 10g, Protein: 15.3g, Sodium: 65mg, Total Carbs: 46.7g, Dietary Fiber: 9g, Net Carbs: 37.7g

4. PUMPKIN PUREE PORRIDGE

Preparation time: 1 minute

Cooking time: 20 minutes

Servings: 1

Ingredients:

- 1-cup water
- 1/3-cup rolled oats
- 1-Tbsp chia seeds
- 1-Tbsp cocoa powder, unsweetened
- ½-tsp cinnamon
- ½-pc banana, ripe, sliced
- ¼-cup pumpkin puree
- ¼-tsp vanilla extract
- ¼-cup egg whites

Directions:

5. In a small pot, pour a cup of water, and bring it to a boil. Upon boiling, add in the

oats, chia seeds, cocoa powder, and cinnamon. Stir well until thoroughly combined. Cover the pot. Bring to a simmer for a minute.

6. Add in the banana, and cook further for 5 minutes. Stir periodically to break up the banana slices. As soon as the mixture absorbs about a quarter of the water, pour in the pumpkin puree. Stir the mixture slowly, and cook further for a couple of minutes.

7. As the mixture absorbs the water almost entirely, add the vanilla and egg whites. Whisk for about 3 minutes until thoroughly combined. Return the lid on the pot and cook for 5 minutes more.

8. Serve hot with your choice of toppings.

Nutrition: Calories: 197, Fat: 6.5g, Protein: 9.8g, Sodium: 10mg, Total Carbs: 33g, Dietary Fiber: 8.4g, Net Carbs: 24.6g

9. CHOCO CHIA BANANA BOWL

Preparation time: 4 hours, 5 minutes

Cooking time: 0 minutes

Servings: 3

Ingredients:

- ½-cup chia seeds
- 1-pc large banana, very ripe
- ½-tsp pure vanilla extract
- 2-cups almond milk, unsweetened
- 1-Tbsp cacao powder
- 2-Tbsps raw honey or maple syrup
- 2-Tbsps cacao nibs
- 2-Tbsps chocolate chips
- 1-pc large banana, sliced

Directions:

1. Combine the chia seeds and banana in a mixing bowl. By using a fork, mash the banana and mix well until thoroughly combined. Pour in the vanilla and almond milk. Whisk until no more lumps appear.
2. Pour half of the mix into a glass container, and cover it. Add the cacao and syrup to the remaining half mixture in the bowl. Mix well until incorporated. Pour this mixture into another glass container, and cover it. Refrigerate overnight both containers, or for at least 4 hours.
3. To serve, layer the chilled chia puddings equally in three serving bowls. Alternate the layers with the ingredients for mixing-in.

Tips:

You can store the chia puddings or the assembled meal in your refrigerator for up to 5 days.

Nutrition: Calories: 293, Fat: 9.7g, Protein: 14.6g, Sodium: 35mg, Total Carbs: 43.1g, Dietary Fiber: 6.5g, Net Carbs: 36.6g

10. BLUEBERRY BREAKFAST BLEND

Preparation time: 8 minutes

Cooking time: 0 minutes

Servings: 1

Ingredients:

- 1/3-tsp turmeric
- ½-cup spinach
- ¾-cup fresh blueberries
- 1-cup fresh pineapple chunks
- 1-cup water
- 1-Tbsp chia seeds
- 1-Tbsp lemon juice

Directions:

1. Combine all the ingredients in your blender. Blend to a smooth consistency.

Nutrition: Calories: 260, Fat: 8.6g, Protein: 13g, Sodium: 30mg, Total Carbs: 39.5g, Dietary Fiber: 7g, Net Carbs: 32.5g

11. QUICK QUINOA WITH CINNAMON & CHIA

Preparation time: 15 minutes

Cooking time: 3 minutes

Servings: 2

Ingredients:

- 2-cups quinoa, pre-cooked
- 1-cup cashew milk
- ½-tsp ground cinnamon
- 1-cup fresh blueberries
- ¼-cup walnuts, toasted
- 2-tsps raw honey
- 1-Tbsp chia seeds

Directions:

1. In a saucepan placed over medium-low heat, add the quinoa and cashew milk. Stir in the cinnamon, blueberries, and walnuts. Cook slowly for three minutes.
2. Remove the pan from the heat. Stir in the honey. Garnish with chia seeds on top before serving.

Nutrition: Calories: 887, Fat: 29.5g, Protein: 44.3g, Sodium: 85mg, Total Carbs: 129.3g, Dietary Fiber: 18.5g, Net Carbs: 110.8g

12. PLUM, PEAR & BERRY-BAKED BROWN RICE RECIPE

Preparation time: 12 minutes

Cooking time: 30 minutes

Servings: 2

Ingredients:

- 1-cup water

- ½-cup brown rice
- A pinch of cinnamon
- ½-tsp pure vanilla extract
- 2-Tbsps pure maple syrup (divided)
- Sliced fruits: berries, pears, or plums
- A pinch of salt (optional)

Directions:

1. Preheat your oven at 400°F.
2. Bring the water and brown rice mixture to a boil in a pot placed over medium-high heat. Stir in the cinnamon and vanilla extract. Reduce the heat to medium-low. Simmer for 18 minutes, or until the brown rice is tender.
3. Fill two oven-safe bowls with equal portions of the rice. Pour a tablespoon of maple syrup into each bowl. Top the bowls with the sliced fruits and sprinkle over a pinch of salt.
4. Put the bowls in the oven. Bake for 12 minutes, or until the fruits start caramelizing and the syrup begins bubbling.

Nutrition: Calories: 227, Fat: 6.3g, Protein: 14.1g, Sodium: 80mg, Total Carbs: 32.2g, Dietary Fiber: 3.6g, Net Carbs: 28.6g

13. GOOD GRAINS WITH CRANBERRIES & CINNAMON

Preparation time: 8 minutes

Cooking time: 35 minutes

Servings: 2

Ingredients:

- 1-cup of grains (choice of amaranth, buckwheat, or quinoa)
- 2½-cups coconut water or almond milk
- 1-stick cinnamon
- 2-pcs whole cloves
- 1-pc star anise pod (optional)
- Fresh fruit: apples, blackberries, cranberries, pears, or persimmons
- Maple syrup (optional)

Directions:

1. Bring the grains, coconut water, and spices to a boil in a covered saucepan. Reduce the heat to medium-low. Simmer for 25 minutes, or until the grains are tender.
2. To serve, discard the spices and top with fruit slices. If desired, drizzle with the maple syrup.

Nutrition: Calories: 628, Fat: 20.9g, Protein: 31.4g, Sodium: 96mg, Total Carbs: 112.3g, Dietary Fiber: 33.8g, Net Carbs: 78.5g

14. SEARED SYRUPY SAGE PORK PATTIES

Preparation time: 12 minutes

Cooking time: 10 minutes

Servings: 2

Ingredients:

- 2-lbs ground pork, pastured
- 3-Tbsps maple syrup, grade B
- 3-Tbsps minced fresh sage
- ¾-tsp sea salt
- ½-tsp garlic powder
- 1-tsp solid cooking fat

Directions:

1. Break the ground pork into chunks in a mixing bowl. Drizzle evenly with the maple syrup. Sprinkle with the spices. Mix well until thoroughly combined. Form the mixture into eight patties. Set aside.
2. Heat the fat in a cast-iron skillet placed over medium heat. Cook the patties for 10 minutes on each side, or until browned.

Nutrition: Calories: 405, Fat: 11.2g, Protein: 30.3g, Sodium: 240mg, Total Carbs: 53.3g, Dietary Fiber: 0.8g, Net Carbs: 45.5g

15. WAFFLES WHIPPED WITH PERFECT PLANTAIN PAIR

Preparation time: 12 minutes

Cooking time: 10 minutes

Servings: 2

Ingredients:

- 2-cups large plantains, medium-ripe, peeled and sliced
- 2½-Tbsps coconut oil, melted
- 1-tsp apple cider vinegar
- 1-tsp pure vanilla extract
- 1-tsp cinnamon
- ½-tsp baking soda
- ½-tsp sea salt
- Choice of fresh fruit, maple syrup, and whipped coconut cream for serving

Directions:

1. Preheat your waffle iron to level 5 on its dial.
2. Combine the plantain and oil in your blender. Puree to a smooth consistency. Add the apple cider vinegar, vanilla, and cinnamon. Blend again on high speed until thoroughly combined. Add the baking soda and salt. By using a spatula, stir the mixture until forming a batter. Set aside.
3. Grease your waffle iron and pour 1/3 cup of the batter. Cook until the waffle turns brown to your liking.
4. Repeat until forming the batter. Ensure to grease the iron before pouring the batter. Stack the cooked waffles on a wire rack.
5. To serve, top each waffle with fresh fruit of your choice. Drizzle with the syrup, and then, garnish with the whipped coconut cream.

Tips:

The best plantain waffles should have a variety of ripeness. The riper plantain contributes to a sweeter flavor, while the other adds a starchy blend to hold them together.

Nutrition: Calories: 805, Fat: 26.8g, Protein: 40.2g, Sodium: 478mg, Total Carbs: 108.6g, Dietary Fiber: 8g, Net Carbs: 100.6g

16. TURKEY WITH THYME & SAGE SAUSAGE

Preparation time: 40 minutes

Cooking time: 25 minutes

Servings: 4

Ingredients:

- 1-lb ground turkey
- ½-tsp cinnamon
- ½-tsp garlic powder
- 1-tsp fresh rosemary
- 1-tsp fresh thyme
- 1-tsp sea salt
- 2-tsps fresh sage
- 2-Tbsps coconut oil

Directions:

1. Stir in all the ingredients, except for the oil, in a mixing bowl. Refrigerate overnight, or for 30 minutes.
2. Pour the oil into the mixture. Form the mixture into four patties.
3. In a lightly greased skillet placed over medium heat, cook the patties for 5 minutes on each side, or until their middle portions are no longer pink. You can also cook them by baking in the oven for 25 minutes at 400°F.

Nutrition: Calories: 284, Fat: 9.4g, Protein: 14.2g, Sodium: 290mg, Total Carbs: 36.9g, Dietary Fiber: 0.7g, Net Carbs: 36.2g

17. SWEET AND SAVORY BREAKFAST HASH

Preparation time: 10 minutes

Cooking time: 15 minutes

Servings: 2

Ingredients:

For the turkey:

- ¼ tsp cinnamon
- ¼ tsp thyme (dried)

- ½ tbsp coconut oil
- ½ lb. ground turkey
- Sea salt

For the hash:

- ¼ tsp garlic powder
- ¼ tsp thyme (dried)
- ¼ tsp turmeric
- 1/3 tsp ginger (powdered)
- ½ tsp cinnamon
- ½ tbsp coconut oil
- ¼ cup of carrots (shredded)
- 1 cup of butternut squash (cubed, you can also use sweet potato)
- 1 cup of spinach (you can also use other types of greens)
- ½ onion (chopped)
- 1 small apple (peeled, cored, chopped)
- 1 small zucchini (chopped)
- Sea salt

Directions:

1. In a skillet, heat half of the coconut oil over medium-high heat.
2. Add the turkey and cook until it's browned.
3. While cooking, season the meat with the spices and mix well.
4. Once cooked, move the turkey onto a plate.
5. Add the remaining coconut oil into the skillet, along with the onion.
6. Sauté the onion until softened for about 2 to 3 minutes.
7. Add the apple, carrots, squash, and zucchini and cook until softened for about 4 to 5 minutes.
8. Add the spinach and continue cooking until the leaves wilt.
9. Add the cooked turkey, along with the hash seasonings, then continue mixing. Taste the hash and adjust the seasonings according to your taste.
10. Spoon the hash onto plates and serve.

Nutrition: Calories: 1284, Fat: 103.02g, Protein: 62.02g, Sodium: 184mg, Total Carbs: 28.23g

18. 5-MINUTE AVOCADO TOAST

Preparation time: 5 minutes

Cooking time: 0 minutes

Servings: 1

Ingredients:

- ½ tsp lemon juice (freshly squeezed)
- 1 tbsp celery (chopped)
- ¼ avocado
- 1 hard-boiled egg (chopped, you can also use 1/3 cup of cubed tofu or store-bought egg replacers)
- 1 slice of toast (whole-wheat)
- Salt

Directions:

1. In a bowl, add the avocado and mash well.
2. Add the lemon juice, celery, and salt, then mix until well incorporated.
3. Fold in the egg until just combined.
4. Spread the mixture on the slice of toast.
5. Enjoy!

Nutrition: Calories: 160, Fat: 12.7g, Protein: 7.36g, Sodium: 72mg, Total Carbs: 5.25g

19. HEALTHY CHICKPEA SCRAMBLE STUFFED SWEET POTATOES

Preparation time: 5 minutes

Cooking time: 20 minutes

Servings: 2

Ingredients:

For the scramble:

- ½ tsp avocado oil
- ½ tsp turmeric
- 1 cup of chickpeas (soaked overnight, boiled for an hour, drained, and dried; you can also use canned, but you must first rinse, drain, and dry)
- ¼ small onion (diced)

- 2 cloves of garlic (minced)
- Sea salt

For the kale:

- ½ tsp avocado oil
- ½ tsp garlic (minced)
- 1 cup of kale leaves (stems removed, cut into small pieces)

For assembling:

- ½ avocado (sliced)
- 2 small sweet potatoes (baked)

Directions:

1. In a pan, add the avocado oil over medium heat, along with the garlic and onions.
2. Cook for about 3 to 4 minutes until softened.
3. Add the chickpeas, turmeric, and salt, then continue cooking for about 10 minutes. To avoid drying the mixture out, you may add teaspoons of water.
4. Mash about 2/3 of the chickpeas using a wooden spoon to make a scrambled texture.
5. Take the pan off the heat and set it aside.
6. In a separate pan, add the avocado oil over medium heat, along with the garlic and kale.
7. Cook for about 5 minutes, until soft, then take the pan off the heat.
8. Slice one baked sweet potato in half and use a spoon to scoop out the center.
9. Spoon half of the chickpea scramble into the baked sweet potato and top with half of the softened kale.
10. Top with half of the avocado slices.
11. Repeat the assembling steps for the other baked sweet potato.
12. Serve and enjoy.

Nutrition: Calories: 275, Fat: 11.76g, Protein: 8.31g, Sodium: 190mg, Total Carbs: 37.34g

20. HIGH-PROTEIN: BREAKFAST BOWL

Preparation time: 5 minutes

Cooking time: 0 minutes

Servings: 1

Ingredients for the breakfast bowl:

- 1 ½ tbsp plant-based Protein: powder
- ¼ cup of blueberries
- ¼ cup of raspberries
- 1 small banana (sliced)
- 1 small sweet potato (baked)

Ingredients for the topping:

- Chia seeds
- Hemp hearts
- Other toppings of your choice

Directions:

1. Scoop out the flesh of the baked sweet potato and place it in a bowl.
2. Use a fork to mash the flesh until you get the consistency you desire.
3. Add the Protein: powder and mix until well combined.
4. Arrange the blueberries, raspberries, and banana slices in layers on top of the mashed sweet potato.
5. Top with your desired toppings.
6. Serve while warm or chill in the refrigerator for about 15 minutes before serving.

Nutrition: Calories: 290, Fat: 0.85g, Protein: 10.36g, Sodium: 190mg, Total Carbs: 65.13g

21. GREEN SMOOTHIE BOWL

Preparation time: 10 minutes

Cooking time: 0 minutes

Servings: 2

Ingredients:

- 1 cup of fresh strawberries, hulled
- 2 medium ripe bananas, (previously sliced and frozen)
- ¼ of a ripe avocado (peeled, pitted, and chopped)
- 1 cup of fresh spinach
- 1 cup of fresh kale, trimmed
- 1 tablespoon of flaxseed meal
- 1 ½ cups of unsweetened almond milk
- ¼ cup of almonds (toasted and chopped)
- ¼ cup of unsweetened coconut, shredded

Direction:

1. Put all ingredients into a high-speed blender except almonds and coconut. Pulse to smoothen.
2. Transfer the puree to bowls and serve immediately with almonds and coconut toppings.

Nutrition: Calories: 352, Fats: 18.6g, Carbs: 45.3g, Sugar: 19.3g, Proteins: 7.9g, Sodium: 168mg

22. FRUITY BOWL

Preparation time: 10 minutes

Cooking time: 0 minutes

Servings: 2

Ingredients:

- 2 cups of frozen cherries (pitted)
- 4 dates (pitted and chopped)
- 1 large apple (peeled, cored, and chopped)
- A cup of fresh cherries pitted
- 2 tablespoons of Chia seeds

Directions:

1. Put frozen cherries and dates in a high-speed blender and pulse.
2. Mix the chopped apple with fresh cherries and Chia seeds in a bowl.
3. Add cherry sauce to the puree and stir.
4. Cover and refrigerate them overnight before serving.

Nutrition: Calories: 211, Fats: 3.2g, Carbs: 49.7g, Sugar: 35g, Proteins: 3.8g, Sodium: 6mg

23. QUINOA & PUMPKIN PORRIDGE

Preparation time: 10 minutes

Cooking time: 12 minutes

Servings: 4

Ingredients:

- 3½ cups of filtered water
- 1¾ cups of quinoa (soaked for fifteen minutes and rinsed)
- 14 ounces of unsweetened coconut milk
- 1¾ cups of sugar-free pumpkin puree
- 2 teaspoons of ground cinnamon
- 1 teaspoon of ground ginger
- A pinch of ground cloves
- A pinch of ground nutmeg
- Salt
- 3 tablespoons of extra-virgin coconut oil
- 4-6 drops of liquid stevia
- 1 teaspoon of organic vanilla flavor

Directions:

1. Pour water and quinoa into a pan and cook on high heat.
2. Cover the pan and let the produce boil.
3. Reduce heat to low and simmer for around 12 minutes or until all liquid gets absorbed.
4. Add the remaining ingredients and stir thoroughly.
5. Immediately, remove switch off the cooker, and serve warm.

Nutrition: Calories: 561, Fats: 29g, Carbs: 60.3g, Sugar: 6.2g, Proteins: 13g, Sodium: 80mg

24. APPLE OMELET

Preparation time: 5 minutes

Cooking time: 10 minutes

Servings: 1

Ingredients:

- 2 large organic eggs
- 1/8 teaspoon of organic vanilla flavoring
- A Pinch of salt
- 2 teaspoons of coconut oil, divided
- ½ apple fruit (cored and sliced)
- ¼ teaspoon of ground cinnamon
- 1/8 teaspoon of ground ginger
- 1/8 teaspoon of ground nutmeg

Directions:

1. Combine eggs with vanilla flavoring and salt in a bowl. Stir the mixture to obtain a fluffy texture and set aside.
2. Melt one teaspoon of coconut oil in a non-stick pan over medium-low heat.
3. Sprinkle the apple slices and spices in a layered manner.
4. Cook for around 4-5 minutes while flipping.
5. Add the residual oil to the skillet.
6. Add the egg mixture over apple slices evenly.
7. Tilt the pan to spread the egg mixture evenly.
8. Cook for around 3-4 minutes.
9. Transfer the omelet to a wide plate and serve.

Nutrition: Calories: 284, Fats: 19.3g, Carbs: 17g, Sugar: 12.5g, Proteins: 12.9g, Sodium: 296mg

CHAPTER 8. LUNCH

25. BALSAMIC SALMON SPINACH SALAD

Preparation time: 10 minutes

Cooking time: 0 minutes

Servings: 4

Ingredients:

- 2 salmon fillets (6 ounces each)
- 6 cups fresh baby spinach
- 2 tbsps. chopped walnuts
- 2 tbsps. dried cranberries
- 4 tbsps. balsamic vinaigrette, divided
- ½ cup cubed avocado
- 2 tbsps. sunflower kernels
- Olive oil cooking spray

Directions:

1. Spray a broiler pan with some cooking spray.
2. Place salmon in the pan. Trickle half the vinaigrette over the salmon.
3. Set up your oven to broil mode. Place the rack about 4 inches away from the heating element and preheat the oven.
4. Place the broiler pan in the oven and broil for 10 to 14 minutes or until cooked through.
5. Cut each salmon into two equal portions.
6. Place spinach in a bowl. Drizzle remaining vinaigrette over it. Toss well.
7. Take four plates and divide equally the spinach among the plates.
8. Place a piece of salmon on each plate. Scatter avocado, sunflower kernels, walnuts, and cranberries on top and serve.

Nutrition: Calories: 265, Fat: 18 g, Total Carbohydrate: 10 g, Protein: 18 g

26. MEDITERRANEAN TUNA-SPINACH SALAD

Preparation time: 10 minutes

Cooking time: 0 minutes

Servings: 4

Ingredients:

For the dressing:

- 6 tbsps. tahini
- 6 tbsps. water
- 6 tbsps. lemon juice

For the salad:

- 4 cans (5 ounces each) chunk light tuna in water, drained
- ½ cup feta cheese
- 8 cups baby spinach
- 16 kalamata olives, pitted, chopped
- ½ cup chopped parsley
- 4 medium oranges, peeled

Directions:

1. To make the dressing: Combine lemon juice, tahini, and water in a bowl. Whisk until smooth and well combined.
2. Stir in olives, tuna, parsley, and feta.
3. Divide spinach into four serving plates. Place the salad over the spinach and serve with orange.

Nutrition: Calories: 376, Fat: 13.9 g, Total Carbohydrate: 26.2 g, Protein: 25.7 g

27. CHICKEN STIR-FRY

Preparation time: 15 Minutes

Cooking time: 15 Minutes

Servings: 4

Ingredients:

- 2 cups white rice
- 4 cups water
- ⅔ cup soy sauce
- ¼ cup brown sugar
- 1 tablespoon cornstarch
- 1 tablespoon minced fresh ginger
- 1 tablespoon minced garlic
- ¼ teaspoon red pepper flakes
- 3 skinless, boneless chicken breast halves, thinly sliced
- 1 tablespoon sesame oil
- 1 green bell pepper, cut into matchsticks
- 1 (8 ounce) can sliced water chestnuts, drained
- 1 head broccoli, broken into florets
- 1 cup sliced carrots
- 1 onion, cut into large chunks
- 1 tablespoon sesame oil

Directions:

1. Bring rice and water to a boil in a saucepan over high heat. Reduce heat to medium-low, cover, and simmer until rice is tender, and liquid has been absorbed, 20 to 25 minutes.
2. Combine soy sauce, brown sugar, and corn starch in a small bowl; stir until smooth. Mix ginger, garlic, and red pepper into sauce; coat chicken with marinade and refrigerate for at least 15 minutes.
3. Heat 1 tablespoon sesame oil in a large skillet over medium-high heat. Cook and stir bell pepper, water chestnuts, broccoli, carrots, and onion until just tender, about 5 minutes. Remove vegetables from skillet and keep warm.
4. Remove chicken from marinade, reserving liquid. Heat 1 tablespoon sesame oil in skillet over medium-high heat. Cook and stir chicken until slightly pink on the inside, about 2 minutes per side; return vegetables and reserved marinade to skillet. Bring to a boil; cook and stir until chicken is no longer pink in the middle and vegetables are tender, 5 to 7 minutes. Serve over rice.

Nutrition:

Calories: 363; Total Fat: 22g; Total Carbs: 7g; Sugar: 2g; Fiber: 2g; Protein: 36g; Sodium: 993mg

28. GROUND TURKEY AND SPINACH STIR-FRY

Preparation time 10 minutes

Cooking time 10 minutes

Servings: 4

Ingredients:

- 1 tbs sesame oil
- 1 lb. Ground Turkey
- ½ cup diced Onion
- 2 tbs Fish Sauce
- 1 tbs Minced Garlic
- 1 tbs Ginger Powder or 1 tsp of Fresh Finely Chopped Ginger
- 3 tbs Soy Sauce
- 1 tbs Sriracha
- 1 tbs coconut palm sugar or brown sugar
- 4 cups of Fresh Spinach
- Serve over cooked brown rice.

Directions:

1. In a sauté pan, add sesame oil, ground turkey, diced onion, fish sauce, fresh garlic, fresh ginger, Sriracha sauce, Coconut Palm Sugar (or Brown Sugar) and 2 tbs of Soy Sauce.
2. Brown until fully cooked mixing in the ingredients.
3. Add fresh spinach and 1 tbs of Soy Sauce.
4. Stir fry together until fully cooked. Serve over rice or cauliflower rice.

Nutrition: Calories: 424; Total Fat: 20g; Total Carbs: 9g; Sugar: 3g; Fiber: 2g; Protein: 51g; Sodium: 1,016mg

29. MANGO CHICKEN MEAL

Preparation time: 25 minutes

Cooking time: 10 minutes

Servings: 4

Ingredients

- 2 medium mangoes, peeled and sliced
- 10-ounce coconut almond milk
- 4 teaspoons of vegetable oil
- 4 teaspoons of spicy curry paste
- 14-ounce chicken breast halves, skinless and boneless, cut into cubes
- 4 medium shallots
- 1 large English cucumber, sliced and seeded

Directions:

1. Slice half of the mangoes and add the halves to a bowl.
2. Add mangoes and coconut almond milk to a blender and blend until you have a smooth puree.
3. Keep the mixture on the side.
4. Take a large-sized pot and place it over medium heat, add oil and allow the oil to heat up.
5. Add curry paste and cook for 1 minute until you have a nice fragrance; add shallots and chicken to the pot and cook for 5 minutes.
6. Pour mango puree into the mix and allow it to heat up.
7. Serve the cooked chicken with mango puree and cucumbers.
8. Enjoy!

Nutrition:

Calories: 398, Fat: 20g, Carbohydrates: 32g, Protein: 26g

30. SWEET POTATO PLATTER

Preparation time: 5 minutes

Cooking time: 7-8 hours

Servings: 4

Ingredients

- 6 sweet potatoes, washed and dried

Directions:

1. Loosely ball up 7-8 pieces of aluminum foil in the bottom of your Slow Cooker, covering about half of the surface area.
2. Prick each potato 6-8 times using a fork.
3. Wrap each potato with foil and seal them.
4. Place wrapped potatoes in the cooker on top of the foil bed.
5. Place lid and cook on LOW for 7-8 hours.
6. Use tongs to remove the potatoes and unwrap them.
7. Serve and enjoy!

Nutrition: Calories: 129, Fat: 0g, Carbohydrates: 30g, Protein: 2g

31. SALTY CARAMEL DIP

Preparation time: 5 minutes

Cooking time: 0 minutes

Servings: 2

Ingredients:

- 1 cup soft Medjool date, pitted
- 1 teaspoon vanilla extract
- ¼ cup almond milk
- 1 teaspoon fresh lemon juice
- 1 tablespoon coconut oil
- ¼ teaspoon salt

Directions:

1. Add all ingredients to your blender.
2. Pulse until you get a smooth mixture.
3. Serve chilled and enjoy!

Nutrition: Calories: 113, Fat: 7.2g, Carbohydrates: 11.2g, Protein: 0.4g

32. ANTI-INFLAMMATORY TURMERIC GUMMIES

Preparation time: 4 hours

Cooking time: 10 minutes

Servings: 6

Ingredients:

- 1 teaspoon turmeric, grounded
- 8 tablespoons gelatin powder, unflavored
- 6 tablespoons maple syrup
- 3 ½ cups of water

Directions:

1. Take a pot and combine maple syrup, turmeric, and water.
2. Bring it to boil for 5 minutes.
3. Remove from the heat and sprinkle with gelatin powder.
4. Mix to hydrate the gelatin.
5. Then turn on the heat again and bring to a boil till the gelatin dissolves properly.
6. Take a dish and pour the mixture.
7. Let it chill for 4 hours in your refrigerator.
8. Slice and serve.
9. Enjoy!

Nutrition: Calories: 68, Fat: 0.03g, Carbohydrates: 17g, Protein: 0.2g

33. DELICIOUS SNOW CRAB

Preparation time: 10 minutes

Cooking time: 10 minutes

Servings: 2

Ingredients:

- 2 clusters Snow Crab legs
- 1/2 cup melted butter
- 1 tablespoon Old Bay seasoning
- 1 lemon cut into wedges

Directions:

How to Boil Crab Legs

1. Fill a large pot with water and bring to a boil. Season the water with 1 tablespoon of salt, if desired. Submerge crab legs into the boiling water and simmer for 5 minutes. Remove from water and serve with melted butter, Old Bay seasoning, and lemon wedges for squeezing over meat.

How to Steam Crab Legs

2. Bring a large pot of water to a boil. Place a steamer basket over the boiling water. Place crab legs in steamer basket. Put lid on to cover and steam 5-7 minutes. Remove and serve with melted butter, Old Bay seasoning, and lemon wedges for squeezing over meat.

How to Broil Crab Legs in the Oven

3. Preheat your oven on the broiler setting. Place crab legs on a baking sheet. Brush legs with melted butter or olive oil, if desired. Place tray 6 to 8 inches beneath the broiler and broil 3 to 4 minutes per side flipping halfway through. Serve hot with melted butter, Old Bay seasoning, and lemon wedges for squeezing over meat.

Nutrition: Calories: 643, Fat: 51g, Carbohydrates: 3g, Protein: 41g

34. CHICKEN LETTUCE WRAPS

Preparation time: 20 minutes

Cooking time: 0 minutes

Servings: 4

Ingredients:

- 2 heads butter lettuce
- 1 lb. chicken breast, boneless, grilled, and cut ½ inch cubes
- ½ cup radishes, thinly sliced
- 1 cup shredded carrots
- 2 scallions, sliced
- 2 tablespoon cilantro, fresh
- 3 tablespoon squeezed lime juice, fresh
- 1 teaspoon lime zest
- ½ cup sesame oil, toasted
- 1 garlic clove

- 3 tablespoon coconut aminos
- 1 ginger, freshly sliced
- 1 tablespoon sesame seeds

Directions:

1. Place the lettuce leaves on a plate then equally divide the chicken, radishes, carrots, scallions, and cilantro among them.
2. Add lime juice, lime zest oil, garlic, coconut aminos, and ginger in a blender. Blend until smooth.
3. Drizzle the dressing from the blender on the chicken and veggies then sprinkle with sesame seeds.
4. Serve.

Nutrition: Calories 342, Total Fat: 30 g, Carbs: 13 g, Protein: 7g

35. CHICKEN BREAST WITH CHERRY SAUCES

Preparation time: 10 minutes

Cooking time: 30 minutes

Servings: 4

Ingredients

- 1 tablespoon coconut oil
- 4 chicken breasts, boneless and skinless
- Salt
- Black pepper, freshly ground
- 2 scallions, sliced
- 1 tablespoon balsamic vinegar
- ½ cup cherries, dried
- ¼ cup chicken broth

Directions:

1. Preheat your oven at 375F
2. Meanwhile, melt oil on an oven-safe skillet over medium heat.

3. Season the chicken with salt and pepper then place it on the skillet. Brown it on both sides for 3 minutes per side.
4. Add scallions, vinegar, cherries, and chicken broth. Cover the skillet and place it in the preheated oven.
5. Bake for 20 minutes or until the chicken is well cooked. Serve.

Nutrition: Calories: 379, Total Fat: 14 g, Carbs: 17 g, Protein: 43g

36. BLACK RICE BOWL WITH TAHINI, PISTACHIOS, AND RASPBERRIES

Preparation time: 15 minutes

Cooking time: 25 minutes

Servings: 4

Ingredients:

- 1 ½ cups black rice, cleaned and rinsed
- ½ teaspoon kosher salt
- 3 cups water
- 1 cup raspberries, fresh
- ½ cup roasted pistachios, chopped and lightly salted
- ½ cup tahini
- 1 teaspoon raw honey
- 1 cup coconut milk
- Mint leaves, fresh

Directions:

1. Put rice, salt, and water into a pot and bring it to a boil over medium heat.
2. Reduce the heat to low and cook the rice covered for about 25 minutes until all the water is absorbed.
3. Transfer the rice to the platter and top with raspberries, pistachios, tahini, honey, milk, and mint leaves.
4. Serve and enjoy.

Nutrition: Calories: 516, Total Fat: 34g, Carbs: 55g, Protein: 17g

37. BAKED SWEET POTATOES

Preparation time: 5 minutes

Cooking time: 25 minutes

Servings: 4

Ingredients:

- 15-ounce chickpeas, rinsed and drained
- ½ teaspoon olive oil
- 4 sweet potatoes, rinsed and cut lengthwise
- ½ teaspoon cumin
- ½ teaspoon coriander
- ½ teaspoon cinnamon
- ½ teaspoon smoked paprika

Garlic Herb Sauce:

- ¼ cup hummus
- ½ lemon, juiced
- 1 teaspoon dried dill
- 3 minced garlic cloves
- Unsweetened almond milk

Directions:

1. Preheat the oven at 400°F.
2. Line a baking sheet with a foil then set it aside.
3. Put the chickpeas, ¼ tablespoon olive oil, and spices into a bowl and toss to coat.
4. Transfer the chickpeas to a baking sheet.
5. Rub the sweet potatoes with the remaining olive oil and place them on the baking sheet with the cut side down.
6. Bake the sweet potatoes for 25 minutes.
7. Meanwhile, prepare the garlic sauce by whisking all the sauce ingredients in a bowl. Add enough almond milk so that it is pourable.
8. Once the sweet potatoes are done, transfer them to a platter with the fresh side up.
9. Top the sweet potatoes with garlic sauce and serve while hot.

Nutrition: Calories: 308, Total Fat: 6g, Carbs: 55g, Protein: 11g

38. GRILLED SAUERKRAUT AVOCADO SANDWICH

Preparation time: 10 minutes

Cooking time: 16 minutes

Servings: 4

Ingredients:

- 8 slices whole-wheat bread
- Olive oil
- 1 cup hummus
- 1 cup sauerkraut, rinsed and squeezed
- 1 avocado, peeled and sliced lengthwise

Directions:

1. Preheat the oven at 450°F and line a baking sheet with a foil then set aside.
2. Spread oil on one side of the bread slices.
3. Place the 4 bread slices on the baking sheet with the oiled side down.
4. Spread half of the hummus on the slices.
5. Place the sauerkraut over the hummus, then top with the avocado slices.
6. Spread the remaining hummus on the remaining bread slices then place them over the avocado with the hummus side down.
7. Bake the slices for 8 minutes on each side.
8. Transfer the sandwich to a platter and serve.

Nutrition: Calories: 319, Total Fat: 14g, Carbs: 39g, Protein: 10g

39. GROUND TURKEY AND SWEET POTATO

Preparation time: 10 minutes

Cooking time: 20 minutes

Servings: 4

Ingredients:

- 2 teaspoons avocado oil
- ½ finely chopped yellow onion
- 1 chopped sweet potato
- 4 minced garlic cloves
- 1 lb. ground turkey
- 2 teaspoons dried oregano
- Salt to taste
- ¼ cup chicken broth
- 3 chopped chives

Directions:

1. Pour oil in a skillet and heat over medium heat.
2. Sauté the onions for 3 minutes stirring often.
3. Stir the sweet potatoes into the skillet and cook covered for about 5 minutes.
4. Scoot the sweet potatoes to the side of the skillet and add the turkey, oregano, and salt.
5. Brown the turkey for about 2 minutes on each side.
6. Mix the sweet potatoes and the turkey then add the chicken broth.
7. Cook the turkey covered for 5 minutes.
8. Uncover the turkey and cook for an additional 2 minutes.
9. Cook for about 1 minute.
10. Serve and enjoy.

Nutrition: Calories: 743, Total Fat: 59g, Carbs: 26g, Protein: 28

40. ZUCCHINI AND GROUND TURKEY

Preparation time: 10 minutes

Cooking time: 20 minutes

Servings: 4

Ingredients:

- 2 teaspoons avocado oil
- 1 lb. ground turkey
- 1 chopped zucchini squash
- 1 ginger, grated
- 3 chopped green onions
- A handful of baby spinach
- 1 teaspoon dried oregano
- 1 teaspoon dried basil
- Sea salt to taste

Directions:

1. Pour the oil into a skillet and heat it over medium heat.
2. Add the turkey to the skillet and brown it for about 4 minutes on each side.
3. Break the turkey into small pieces using a spatula.
4. Stir in the zucchini, ginger, and onions to the turkey and cook covered for 3 minutes.
5. Stir in the spinach, oregano, basil, and salt to the turkey and cook covered for 2 minutes.
6. Stir the turkey and cook for an additional 4 minutes.
7. Transfer the zucchini and the turkey to a platter and serve.

Nutrition: Calories 328, Total Fat: 21g, Carbs: 4g, Protein: 31g

41. POPCORN CHICKEN

Preparation time: 15 minutes

Cooking time: 10 minutes

Servings: 4

Ingredients:

- 1/5 lb. chicken breast halves, boneless and skinless
- ½ teaspoon paprika
- ¼ teaspoon mustard, ground
- ¼ teaspoon of garlic powder
- 3 tablespoons of arrowroot

Directions:

1. Cut the chicken into small pieces and keep it in a bowl.
2. Combine the paprika, garlic powder, mustard, salt, and pepper in another bowl.
3. Reserve a teaspoon of your seasoning mixture. Sprinkle the other portion on the chicken. Coat evenly by tossing.
4. Combine the reserved seasoning and arrowroot in a plastic bag.
5. Combine well by shaking.
6. Keep your chicken pieces in the bag. Seal it and shake for coating evenly.
7. Now transfer the chicken to a mesh strainer. Shake the excess arrowroot.
8. Keep aside for 5-10 minutes. The arrowroot should start to get absorbed into your chicken.
9. Preheat your air fryer at 390°F.
10. Apply some oil to the air fryer basket.
11. Keep the chicken pieces inside. They should not overlap.
12. Apply cooking spray.
13. Cook until the chicken isn't pink anymore.

Nutrition: Calories 156, Total Fat: 4g, Carbs: 6g, Protein: 24g, Sugar: 0g, Fiber: 1g, Cholesterol 65mg, Sodium 493mg

42. SPICY CHICKEN AND CAULIFLOWER

Preparation time: 5 minutes

Cooking time: 25 minutes

Servings: 4

Ingredients:

- 2 pounds chicken breasts, skinless, boneless, and cubed
- 1 tablespoon rice vinegar
- 4 tablespoons raw honey
- 6 tablespoons coconut aminos
- 2 garlic cloves, minced
- 2 pounds cauliflower, florets separated
- ½ cup of water
- 1 tablespoon whole wheat flour
- 2 tablespoons olive oil
- 3 green onions, chopped
- 2 tablespoons sesame seeds

Directions:

1. In a bowl, mix 3 tablespoons of honey with 3 tablespoons of coconut aminos, garlic, vinegar, and the chicken. Heat a pan with half of the oil over medium heat, add cauliflower and stir then cook for 5 minutes and transfer to a bowl. Heat the pan with the rest of the oil over medium heat, Drain the chicken, reserving the marinade, then add it to the pan.
2. Toss and cook for 6 minutes. In a separate bowl, whisk together the rest of the aminos with the remaining honey, water, whole wheat flour, and the reserved marinade. Add over the chicken, cover the pan and cook on low heat for 10 minutes, take off the heat, add the cauliflower and toss.
3. Divide between plates, sprinkle green onions and sesame seeds on top, and serve. Enjoy!

Nutrition: Calories: 250, Total Fat: 4g, Carbs: 10g, Protein: 12g

43. CURRIED SHRIMP AND VEGETABLES

Preparation time: 10 minutes

Cooking time: 15 minutes

Servings: 4

Ingredients:

- 3 tablespoons coconut oil
- 1 onion, sliced
- 2 cups cauliflower, cut into florets
- 1 cup of coconut milk
- 1 tablespoon curry powder
- ¼ cup fresh parsley, chopped
- 1-pound shrimp, tails removed

Directions:

1. In a large skillet, melt the coconut oil over medium-high heat. Add the onion and cauliflower and cook until they are softened.
2. Add coconut milk, curry, and parsley to the skillet. (Add any other spices you like. Turmeric will give you an even bigger anti-inflammatory boost.) Cook for 2–3 more minutes.
3. Stir the shrimp into the skillet and cook until it is opaque.

Nutrition: Calories 332, Total Fat: 22g, Carbs: 11g, Protein: 24g, Sodium 309 mg

44. SHEET PAN ROSEMARY MUSHROOMS

Preparation time: 10 minutes

Cooking time: 15 minutes

Servings: 2

Ingredients:

- 1 cup mushrooms

- 1 teaspoon minced rosemary
- ½ teaspoon of sea salt
- 1 tablespoon sesame oil

Directions:

1. Line the baking tray with baking paper.
2. Slice the mushrooms roughly and put them in the baking tray.
3. Sprinkle mushrooms with minced rosemary, sea salt, and sesame oil.
4. Mix up the vegetables well with the help of the hand palms.
5. Preheat the oven at 360°F.
6. Cook mushrooms for 15 minutes.

Nutrition: Calories 70, Total Fat: 7g, Carbs: 1.5g, Protein: 1.1g, Fiber: 4g

CHAPTER 9. DINNER

45. SHRIMP AND VEGETABLE CURRY

Preparation time: 5 minutes

Cooking time: 10 minutes

Servings: 4

Ingredients:

- 1 sliced onion
- 1 tablespoons of olive oil
- 2 teaspoons of curry powder
- 1 cup of coconut milk
- 1 cauliflower
- 1 lb. shrimp tails

Directions:

1. Add the onion to your oil.
2. Sauté to make it a bit soft.
3. Steam your vegetables in the meantime.
4. Add the curry seasoning, coconut milk, and spices if you want once the onion has become soft.
5. Cook for 2 minutes.
6. Include the shrimp. Cook for 5 minutes.
7. Serve with the steamed vegetables.

Nutrition: Calories 491, Carbohydrates 11g, Cholesterol 208mg, Total Fat: 39g, Protein: 24g, Sugar: 3g, Fiber: 5g, Sodium 309mg

46. VEGETABLE AND CHICKEN STIR FRY

Preparation time: 5 minutes

Cooking time: 15 minutes

Servings: 6

Ingredients:

- 1 tablespoons of olive oil
- chicken breasts
- 3 medium zucchini or yellow squash
- 2 onions
- 1 teaspoon of garlic powder
- 1 broccoli
- 1 teaspoon basil

- 1 teaspoon of pepper and salt

Directions:

1. Chop the vegetables and chicken.
2. Heat your skillet over medium temperature.
3. Pour olive oil and add the chicken. Cook while stirring.
4. Include the seasonings if you want.
5. Add the vegetables. Keep cooking until it gets slightly soft. Add the onions first and broccoli last.

Nutrition: Calories: 183, Carbohydrates: 9g, Cholesterol: 41mg, Total Fat: 11g, Protein: 12g, Sugar: 4g, Fiber: 3g, Sodium: 468mg

47. BLACKENED CHICKEN BREAST

Preparation time: 10 minutes

Cooking time: 15 minutes

Servings: 2

Ingredients:

- 1 chicken breast halves, skinless and boneless
- 1 teaspoon thyme, ground
- 2 teaspoons of paprika
- 2 teaspoons olive oil
- ½ teaspoon onion powder

Directions:

1. Combine the thyme, paprika, onion powder, and salt in your bowl.
2. Transfer the spice mix to a flat plate.
3. Rub olive oil on the chicken breast. Coat fully.
4. Roll the chicken pieces in the spice mixture. Press down, ensuring that all sides have the spice mix.
5. Keep aside for 5 minutes.
6. In the meantime, preheat your air fryer at 360 degrees F.
7. Keep the chicken in the air fryer basket. Cook for 8 minutes.
8. Flip once and cook for another 7 minutes.
9. Transfer the breasts to a plate. Serve after 5 minutes.

Nutrition: Calories: 424, Carbohydrates: 3g, Cholesterol: 198mg, Total Fat: 11g, Protein: 79g, Sugar: 1g, Fiber: 2g, Sodium: 516mg

48. GREEN HUMMUS

Preparation time: 10 minutes

Cooking time: 10 minutes

Servings: 8

Ingredients:

- 1/3 cup lemon juice, fresh
- ¼ cup fresh tarragon or basil, chopped
- ¼ cup tahini
- ½ cup fresh parsley, chopped
- ½ teaspoon salt, more to taste
- 1 large garlic clove, roughly chopped
- 1 to 2 tablespoons water, optional
- 2 tablespoons olive oil, plus more for serving
- 2 green onions, chopped
- Garnish with extra olive oil and a sprinkling of chopped fresh herbs
- 1 can (12-ounce) garbanzo beans,

Directions:

1. Drain and rinse the garbanzo beans
2. Place all ingredients in a blender and puree until smooth and creamy.
3. Transfer to a bowl and adjust seasoning if needed.
4. Serve with pita chips.

Nutrition: Calories 139, Fat 10g, Carbs: 10g, Protein: 4g

49. PARSLEY 'N LEMON KIDNEY BEANS

Preparation time: 10 minutes

Cooking time: 0 minutes

Servings: 6

Ingredients:

- ¼ cup lemon juice (about 1 ½ lemon)
- ¼ cup olive oil
- ¾ cup chopped fresh parsley

- ¾ teaspoon salt
- 1 can (15 ounces) chickpeas, rinsed and drained
- 1 medium cucumber, peeled, seeded, and diced
- 1 small red onion, diced
- 2 cans (15 ounces each) red kidney beans, rinsed and drained
- 2 stalks celery, sliced in half or thirds lengthwise and chopped
- 2 tablespoons chopped fresh dill or mint
- 3 cloves garlic, pressed or minced
- Small pinch red pepper flakes

Directions:

1. Whisk well in a small bowl the pepper flakes, salt, garlic, and lemon juice until emulsified.
2. In a bowl, combine the prepared kidney beans, chickpeas, onion, celery, cucumber, parsley, and dill (or mint).
3. Drizzle salad with the dressing and toss well to coat.
4. Serve and enjoy.

Nutrition: Calories: 345; Fat: 11g; Carbs: 47g; Protein: 16g

50. MOROCCAN SALAD

Preparation time: 10 minutes

Cooking time: 0 minutes

Servings: 10

Ingredients:

- ¼ cup lemon juice
- ¼ teaspoon ground cinnamon
- ½ cup chopped fresh mint
- ½ cup extra-virgin olive oil
- 1 15-ounce can chickpeas, rinsed
- 1 cup finely diced carrot
- 1 small clove garlic, peeled and minced
- 1 teaspoon kosher salt, divided
- 1½ cups chopped fresh parsley
- 2 15-ounce cans dark red kidney beans, rinsed
- 2 tablespoons ground cumin

Directions:

1. In a salad bowl, whisk well lemon juice, cinnamon, olive oil, garlic, salt, parsley, and cumin.
2. Stir in remaining ingredients and toss well to coat in the dressing.
3. Serve and enjoy.

Nutrition: Calories: 196, Fat: 6g, Carbs: 27g, Protein: 9g

51. PUMPKIN SOUP

Preparation time: 5 minutes

Cooking time: 20 minutes

Servings: 4

Ingredients:

- tbsps. olive oil
- cloves garlic, peeled, minced
- 2 tsps. chopped fresh thyme leaves
- ½ tsp ground cumin
- ½ tsp ground ginger
- ½ tsp chili powder
- 2 cups low-sodium chicken broth
- 2 tbsps. heavy cream
- 1 tsp kosher salt or to taste
- tsps. maple syrup
- 4 tbsps. pumpkin seeds, to garnish

Directions:

1. Place a soup pot over medium flame. Add olive oil and let it heat.
2. Once the oil is heated, add onion and garlic and sauté for a couple of minutes.
3. Stir in pumpkin puree, salt, ginger, thyme, chili powder, and cumin and mix well. Let it simmer for about 4–5 minutes. Stir often. Turn off the heat.
4. Add maple syrup and heavy cream and stir. Let it cool for a few minutes.
5. Ladle into soup bowls.
6. Garnish with pumpkin seeds and serve.

Nutrition:

Calories: 285, Fat: 18g, Total Carbohydrate: 30g, Protein: 6g

52. HEALTHY SHRIMP AND "GRITS"

Preparation time: 2 minutes

Cooking time: 10 minutes

Servings: 4

Ingredients:

For shrimp:

- lbs. large shrimp, peeled, deveined
- tbsps. olive oil
- 4–6 tablespoons Cajun seasoning
- Salt to taste (optional)

For cauliflower "Grits":

- bags (12 oz each) frozen cauliflower
- tbsps. olive oil
- 2 large cloves garlic, finely chopped
- Salt to taste

Directions:

1. Take a large saucepan and pour enough water to fill the pan by at least 3 inches in height from the bottom of the saucepan.
2. Place the saucepan over medium flame. Place a steamer basket in the saucepan. When the water begins to boil, add cauliflower to the steamer basket.
3. Sprinkle garlic on top of the cauliflower. Cover the saucepan and cook until cauliflower is tender.
4. Turn off the heat and remove the steamer basket from the saucepan.
5. Transfer the cauliflower and garlic into the food processor bowl.
6. Add oil and pulse until you get the preferred consistency.
7. Divide cauliflower "Grits" into four bowls.
8. To cook shrimp: Dry the shrimp by patting it with paper towels. Sprinkle a generous amount of Cajun seasoning all over the shrimp. Make sure that the shrimp are well coated with Cajun seasoning. If the Cajun seasoning contains salt, skip the next step and proceed to step 10.

9. Sprinkle salt over the shrimp.

10. Place a large, cast-iron skillet over medium-high flame. Add oil and let it heat.

11. When the pan is heated, spread shrimp all over the bottom of the pan. Cook until the underside turns slightly pink. Turn the shrimp over and cook the other side until they turn slightly pink. When the shrimp is cooked, transfer the shrimp into the bowl of cauliflower "Grits". Drizzle any cooking liquid over the shrimp.

12. Serve.

Nutrition: Calories: 510, Fat: 33g, Total Carbohydrate: 3g, Protein: 47g

53. CREAMY PESTO CHICKEN

Preparation time: 20 minutes

Cooking time: 20 minutes

Servings: 4

Ingredients:

For chicken:

- ¼ cup balsamic vinegar
- 2 tsps. dried oregano
- ½ tsp salt or to taste
- 2 tsps. olive oil
- 1 tsp minced garlic
- boneless, skinless, chicken breast halves (6 oz each)

For pesto:

- ½ cup loosely packed basil leaves
- ½ tsp salt
- ½ cup packed fresh parsley leaves

- ½ cup canned coconut milk

Directions:

1. To make chicken: Combine balsamic vinegar, oregano, salt, olive oil, and garlic in a bowl. Brush this mixture over the chicken and place the chicken in a baking dish that has been sprayed with cooking spray.
2. To make pesto: Blend basil, salt, and parsley in the food processor until finely chopped.
3. With the blender machine running, pour coconut milk through the feeder tube in a thin drizzle until smooth and well combined.
4. Divide chicken into plates. Place 2 tablespoons of pesto on each plate and serve.

Nutrition: Calories: 261, Fat: 11 g, Total Carbohydrates: 4 g, Protein: 35 g

54. GINGERED VEGETABLE CURRY

Preparation time: 10 minutes

Cooking time: 30 minutes

Servings: 4

Ingredients:

- 2 tsps. olive oil
- 1 medium carrot, cut into ½ inch thick slices
- ½ cup chopped onion
- 1 cup 2-inch-long cut green beans
- 1 cup small cauliflower florets
- 4 tsps. red curry paste
- ½ tsp salt or to taste
- 1 cup cooked or canned chickpeas, rinsed drained

- 4 tsps. grated ginger
- 2 cups unsweetened light coconut milk
- 4 tsps. lime juice

To serve:

- 1 1/3 cups hot cooked brown rice
- 4 tsps. coarsely chopped, roasted peanuts
- ¼ cup chopped fresh cilantro

Directions:

1. Heat oil in a large skillet over a medium flame. Once the oil is heated, add onion and sauté for about a minute.
2. Stir in the carrot and cook until the onion turns pink.
3. Add curry paste, salt, and ginger. Stir-fry constantly for about a minute.
4. Pour coconut milk and stir. When the mixture comes to a boil, stir in the chickpeas, green beans, and cauliflower.
5. Cook on low flame until the veggies are tender and gravy is slightly thick. Do not cover while cooking. Add lemon juice and stir. Turn off the heat.
6. Garnish with cilantro.
7. Serve curry over hot cooked brown rice, garnished with peanuts.

Nutrition: Calories: 259, Fat: 10.8 g, Total Carbohydrate: 34.9 g, Protein: 7.6 g

55. BAKED CHICKEN BREAST WITH LEMON & GARLIC

Preparation time: 5 minutes

Cooking time: 20 to 25 minutes

Servings: 4

Ingredients:

- Juice of 1 lemon
- Zest of 1 lemon
- 1 teaspoon garlic powder
- ½ teaspoon salt
- 1 tablespoons avocado oil
- 2 (8-ounce) boneless, skinless chicken breasts

Directions:

1. Preheat the oven at 375°F.
2. In a small bowl, mix the lemon juice, lemon zest, garlic powder, and salt. Set aside.
3. With a basting brush, spread 1½ tablespoons of avocado oil on the bottom of a glass or ceramic baking dish and brush them thoroughly with the chicken breasts in the dish. Brush the remaining 1½ tablespoons of avocado oil.
4. With the brush, coat the chicken with the lemon-garlic mixture.
5. Bake for 20 to 25 minutes, or until the center of the chicken reaches 165°F on an instant-read thermometer.

Tip: For a little extra flavor, add 1 teaspoon of ground ginger to the lemon-garlic mixture.

Nutrition: Calories: 208; Total Fat: 12g; Saturated Fat: 2g; Cholesterol: 56mg; Carbohydrates: 2g; Fiber: 0g; Protein: 23g

56. PORK TENDERLOIN WITH DIJON-CIDER GLAZE

Preparation time: 5 minutes

Cooking time: 25 minutes

Servings: 4

Ingredients:

- ¼ cup apple cider vinegar
- ¼ cup coconut sugar
- 3 tablespoons Dijon mustard
- 2 teaspoons garlic powder
- Dash salt
- 1 (1½-pound) pork tenderloin

Directions:

1. In a small bowl, stir together the vinegar, coconut sugar, mustard, garlic powder,

and salt until the sugar dissolves. Brush this mixture over the pork loin.

2. Place a grill pan over medium-high heat and add the pork. Sear for 2 minutes per side.
4. Spoon half of the vinegar mixture over the pork and reduce the heat to medium. Cover the pan and cook for 10 minutes.
5. Spoon the remaining vinegar mixture over the pork. Cook for 5 minutes, or until the center of the pork reaches 145°F. Transfer the pork to a plate.
6. Bring the vinegar mixture remaining in the pan to a simmer. Cook for 5 minutes to reduce and thicken.
7. Serve the pork drizzled with the glaze.

Tip: To marinate: combine all the ingredients in a large resealable plastic bag. Turn to coat and refrigerate for up to 3 hours.

Nutrition: Calories: 268; Total Fat: 6g; Saturated Fat: 2g; Cholesterol: 110mg; Carbohydrates: 16g; Fiber: 0g; Protein: 36g

57. NUTTY AND FRUITY AMARANTH

Preparation time: 5 minutes

Cooking time: 25 minutes

Servings: 2

Ingredients:

- 1 medium pear, chopped
- ½ cup blueberries
- 1 teaspoon cinnamon
- 1 tablespoon. raw honey
- ¼ cup pumpkin seeds
- 2 cups of filtered water
- 2/3 cups whole-grain amaranth

Directions:

1. In a nonstick pan with cover, boil water and amaranth. Slow fire to a simmer and continues cooking until liquid is absorbed completely around 25-30 minutes.
2. Turn off the fire.

3. Mix in cinnamon, honey, and pumpkin seeds. Mix well.
4. Pour equally into two bowls.
5. Garnish with pear and blueberries.
6. Serve and enjoy.

Nutrition: Calories 416, Total Fat: 12g, Carbs: 58g, Protein: 14g, Fiber: 7g, Sugar: 23g

58. SALMON AND DILL PÂTÉ

Preparation time: 10 minutes

Cooking time: 8 minutes

Servings: 4

Ingredients:

- 6 ounces cooked salmon, bones and skin removed
- ¼ cup heavy (whipping) cream
- 1 tablespoon chopped fresh dill or 1½ teaspoons dried
- zest of 1 lemon
- ½ teaspoon sea salt

Directions:

1. In a blender or food processor (or in a large bowl using a mixer), combine the salmon, heavy cream, dill, lemon zest, and salt. Blend until smooth.

Nutrition: Calories 197, Total Fat: 11g Carbs: 5g Protein: 15g Sugar: 2g

59. NUTTY AND FRUITY GARDEN SALAD

Preparation time: 10 minutes

Cooking time: 0 minutes

Servings: 2

Ingredients:

- 6 cups baby spinach
- ½ cup chopped walnuts, toasted
- 1 ripe red pear, sliced

- 1 ripe persimmon, sliced
- 1 teaspoon garlic minced
- 1 shallot, minced
- 1 tablespoon extra-virgin olive oil
- 2 tablespoons fresh lemon juice
- 1 teaspoon whole-grain mustard

Directions:

1. Mix well garlic, shallot, oil, lemon juice, and mustard in a large salad bowl.
2. Add spinach, pear, and persimmon. Toss to coat well.
3. To serve, garnish with chopped pecans.

Nutrition: Calories 315, Total Fat: 21g, Carbs: 37g, Protein: 7g, Sugar: 20g, Fiber: 9g

60. BROCCOLI-SESAME STIR-FRY

Preparation time: 10 minutes

Cooking time: 8 minutes

Servings: 4

Ingredients:

- 2 tablespoons extra-virgin olive oil
- 1 teaspoon sesame oil
- 4 cups broccoli florets
- 1 tablespoon grated fresh ginger
- ¼ teaspoon sea salt
- 2 garlic cloves, minced
- 2 tablespoons toasted sesame seeds

Directions:

1. In a large nonstick skillet over medium-high heat, heat the olive oil and sesame oil until they shimmer.
2. Add the broccoli, ginger, and salt. Cook for 5 to 7 minutes, stirring frequently until the broccoli begins to brown.
3. Add the garlic. Cook for 30 seconds, stirring constantly.
4. Remove from the heat and stir in the sesame seeds.

Nutrition: Calories 134, Total Fat: 11g Carbs: 9g Protein: 2g Sugar: 2g

61. LEMONY MUSSELS

Preparation time: 5 minutes

Cooking time: 5 minutes

Servings: 4

Ingredients:

- 1 tablespoon extra-virgin olive oil
- 2 minced garlic cloves
- 2 lbs. scrubbed mussels
- Juice of one lemon

Directions:

1. Put some water in a pot, add mussels, bring with a boil over medium heat, cook for 5 minutes, discard unopened mussels and transfer them with a bowl.
2. In another bowl, mix the oil with garlic and freshly squeezed lemon juice, whisk well, and add over the mussels, toss and serve. Enjoy!

Nutrition: Calories 140, Total Fat: 4g, Carbs: 8 g, Protein: 8 g, Sugars 4g, Sodium 600 mg

62. CHERRIES AND QUINOA

Preparation time: 5 minutes

Cooking time: 10 minutes

Servings: 1

Ingredients:

- 1 teaspoon honey – optional
- ¼ teaspoon ground cinnamon
- ½ teaspoon vanilla extract
- ½ cup dried unsweetened cherries
- ½ cup dry quinoa
- 1 cup of water

Directions:

1. Wash quinoa in a bowl, by rubbing vigorously between your hands. Discard water and repeat rinsing two more times.

2. On medium-high fire, place a medium nonstick skillet.
3. Add cinnamon, vanilla extract, cherries, and quinoa.
4. Bring to a boil and stir occasionally.
5. Once boiling, slow fire to a simmer, cover skillet and cook until all water is absorbed and quinoa is tender around 15 minutes.
6. Turn off the fire and let it stand covered for 10 minutes more.
7. Transfer to a bowl and if using honey, pour and mix. Serve and enjoy.

Nutrition: Calories 386, Total Fat: 5.3g, Carbs: 72.12g, Protein: 13.0g, Fiber: 7.7g

63. CELERY ROOT HASH BROWNS

Preparation time: 10 minutes

Cooking time: 10 minutes

Servings: 4

Ingredients:

- 4 tablespoons coconut oil
- ½ teaspoon sea salt
- 2 to 3 medium celery roots

Directions:

1. Scrub the celery root clean and peel it using a vegetable peeler.
2. Grate the celery root in a food processor or a manual grater.
3. In a skillet, add oil and heat it over medium heat.
4. Place the grated celery root on the skillet and sprinkle with salt.

5. Let it cook for 10 minutes on each side or until the grated celery turns brown.
6. Serve warm.

Nutrition: Calories 161, Total Fat: 3g, Carbs: 35g, Protein: 1.9g, Sugar: 0g, Fiber: 3g

64. BLUEBERRY CHIA PUDDING

Preparation time: 10 minutes

Cooking time: 10 minutes

Servings: 2

Ingredients:

- ½ cup chia seeds
- ½ of frozen banana
- 5 dates (soaked in water)
- 2/3 cup almond milk
- 2 cups frozen blueberries

Directions:

1. Combine the milk, blueberries, dates, and bananas in a blender. Process until the mixture becomes smooth.
2. Transfer the blueberry to a bowl and add the chia seeds.
3. Refrigerate for 30 minutes or overnight if necessary, until the chia seeds form mucilage.
4. Serve with your favorite fruit or nut toppings.

Nutrition: Calories 343, Total Fat: 13g, Carbs: 55g, Protein: 9g, Sugar: 23g, Fiber: 7g

CHAPTER 10. SNACKS

65. OKRA FRIES

Preparation time: 15 minutes

Cooking time: 35 minutes

Servings: 4

Ingredients:

- 2 tablespoons olive oil, divided
- 3 tablespoons creole seasoning
- ½ teaspoon ground turmeric
- 1 teaspoon water
- 1-pound okra, trimmed and slit in the middle

Directions:

1. Preheat the oven at 450 degrees F. Line a baking sheet that has foil paper and grease with 1 tablespoon of oil.
2. In a bowl, mix creole seasoning, turmeric, and water.
3. Fill the slits of okra with turmeric mixture.
4. Place the okra onto a prepared baking sheet in a very single layer.
5. Bake for around 30-35 minutes, flipping once inside the middle way.

Nutrition: Calories: 119, Fat: 6.98g, Carbohydrates: 12.43g, Fiber: 4.6g, Protein: 2.51g, Sodium: 471mg

66. POTATO STICKS

Preparation time: 15 minutes

Cooking time: 10 minutes

Servings: 2

Ingredients:

- 1 large russet potato, peeled and cut into 1/8-inch thick sticks lengthwise
- 10 curry leaves
- ¼ teaspoon ground turmeric
- ¼ teaspoon red chili powder
- Salt, to taste
- 1 tbsp essential olive oil

Directions:

1. Preheat the oven at 400 degrees F. Line 2 baking sheets with parchment papers.
2. In a sizable bowl, add all ingredients and toss to coat well.
3. Transfer the amalgamation into prepared baking sheets in a single layer.
4. Bake for around 10 minutes.
5. Serve immediately.

Nutrition: Calories: 175, Fat: 3.21g, Carbohydrates: 33.78g, Fiber: 2.6g, Protein: 4.06g, Sodium: 79mg

67. ZUCCHINI CHIPS

Preparation time: 15 minutes

Cooking time: 15 minutes

Servings: 2

Ingredients:

- 1 medium zucchini, cut into thin slices
- 1/8 teaspoon ground turmeric
- 1/8 teaspoon ground cumin
- Salt, to taste
- 2 teaspoons essential olive oil

Directions:

1. Preheat the oven at 400 degrees F. Line 2 baking sheets with parchment papers.
2. In a substantial bowl, add all ingredients and toss to coat well.

3. Transfer a combination into prepared baking sheets in a single layer.
4. Bake approximately 10-fifteen minutes.
5. Serve immediately.

Nutrition: Calories: 20, Fat: 2g, Carbohydrates: 0.37g, Fiber: 0.1g, Protein: 0.21g, Sodium: 39mg

68. BEET CHIPS

Preparation time: 15 minutes

Cooking time: 20 minutes

Servings: 2

Ingredients:

- 1 beetroot, trimmed, peeled, and sliced thinly
- 1 teaspoon garlic, minced
- 1 tablespoon nutritional yeast
- ½ teaspoon red chili powder
- 2 teaspoons coconut oil, melted

Directions:

1. Preheat the oven at 375 degrees F. Line a baking sheet using parchment paper.
2. In a large bowl, add all ingredients and toss to coat well.
3. Transfer the mixture into a prepared baking sheet in a very single layer.
4. Bake approximately twenty minutes, flipping once inside the middle way.
5. Serve immediately.

Nutrition: Calories: 80, Fat: 4.5g, Sat Fat: 0.5g, Carbohydrates: 6g, Fiber: 2g, Protein: 3g, Sodium: 300mg

69. SPINACH CHIPS

Preparation time: 10 minutes

Cooking time: 8 minutes

Servings: 1

Ingredients:

- 2 cups fresh spinach leaves
- Few drops of extra-virgin olive oil
- Salt, to taste
- Italian seasoning, to taste

Directions:

1. Preheat the oven at 325 degrees F. Line a baking sheet with parchment paper.
2. In a substantial bowl, add spinach leaves and drizzle with oil.
3. With the hands, rub the spinach leaves till the leaves are coated with oil.
4. Transfer the leaves into a prepared baking sheet in a very single layer.
5. Bake for about 8 minutes.
6. 6. Serve immediately.

Nutrition: Calories: 14, Fat: 4.5g, Sat Fat: 0.23g, Carbohydrates: 2.18g, Fiber: 1.3g, Protein: 1.72g, Sodium: 47mg

70. SWEET & TANGY SEEDS CRACKERS

Preparation time: 15 minutes

Cooking time: 12 hours

Servings: 10

Ingredients:

- 2 cups water
- 1 cup sunflower seeds
- 1 cup flaxseeds

- 1 tablespoon fresh ginger, chopped
- 1 teaspoon raw honey
- ¼ cup freshly squeezed lemon juice
- 1 teaspoon ground turmeric
- Salt, to taste

Directions:

1. In a bowl, add water, sunflower seeds, and flaxseeds and soak for around overnight.
2. Drain the seeds.
3. In a food processor, add soaked seeds and remaining ingredients and pulse till well combined.
4. Set dehydrator at 115 degrees F. Line a dehydrator tray with unbleached parchment paper.
5. Place the mix onto the prepared dehydrator tray evenly.
6. With a knife, score how big crackers.
7. Dehydrate for about 12 hours.

Nutrition: Calories: 176, Fat: 14.32g, Carbohydrates: 8.97g, Fiber: 5.9g, Protein: 6.05g, Sodium: 7mg

71. PLANTAIN CHIPS

Preparation time: quarter-hour

Cooking time: 10 min

Servings: 1

Ingredients:

- 1 plantain, peeled and sliced
- ½ teaspoon ground turmeric
- Salt, to taste
- 1 teaspoon coconut oil, melted

Directions:

1. In a large bowl, add all ingredients and toss to coat well.
2. Transfer the half in the mixture in a large greased bowl.
3. Microwave on high for around 3 minutes.

4. Now, decrease the capacity to 50% and microwave for approximately 2 minutes.
5. Repeat with the remaining plantain mixture.

Nutrition: Calories: 222, Fat: 4.83g, Carbohydrates: 48.98g, Fiber: 3.9g, Protein: 4.36g, Sodium: 8mg

72. QUINOA & SEEDS CRACKERS

Preparation time: 15 minutes

Cooking time: 20 or so minutes

Servings: 6

Ingredients:

- 3 tablespoons water
- 1 tablespoon chia seeds
- 3 tablespoons sunflower seeds
- 1 tablespoon quinoa flour
- 1 teaspoon ground turmeric
- Pinch of ground cinnamon
- Salt, to taste

Directions:

1. Preheat the oven at 345 degrees F. Line a baking sheet with parchment paper.
2. In a bowl, add water and chia seeds and soak for approximately a quarter-hour.
3. After fifteen minutes, add the remaining ingredients and mix well.
4. Spread the mix onto a prepared baking sheet.
5. Bake approximately 20 min.

Nutrition: Calories: 34, Fat: 2.38g, Carbohydrates: 2.35g, Fiber: 0.6g, Protein: 1.21g, Sodium: 1mg

73. APPLE LEATHER

Preparation time: 15 minutes

Cooking time: 12 hours, 25 minutes

Servings: 4

Ingredients:

- 1 cup water
- 8 cups apples, peeled, cored, and chopped
- 1 tablespoon ground cinnamon
- 2 tablespoons freshly squeezed lemon juice

Directions:

1. In a big pan, add water and apples on medium-low heat.
2. Simmer, stirring occasionally for around 10-quarter-hour.
3. Remove from heat and make aside to cool slightly.
4. In a blender, add apple mixture and pulse till smooth.
5. Return the mixture into the pan or medium-low heat.
6. Stir in cinnamon and fresh lemon juice and simmer for approximately 10 minutes.
7. Transfer the mix onto dehydrator trays and with the back of the spoon smooth the very best.
8. Set the dehydrator at 135 degrees F.
9. Dehydrate for around 10-12 hours.
10. Cut the apple leather into equal-sized rectangles.
11. Now, roll each rectangle to make fruit rolls.

Nutrition: Calories: 120, Fat: 0.41g, Carbohydrates: 32.2g, Fiber: 6.3g, Protein: 0.67g, Sodium: 4mg

74. ROASTED CASHEWS

Preparation time: 5 minutes

Cooking time: 20 or so minutes

Servings: 16

Ingredients:

- 2 cups cashews
- 2 teaspoons raw honey
- 1½ teaspoons smoked paprika
- ½ teaspoon chili flakes
- Salt, to taste
- 1 tablespoon freshly squeezed lemon juice
- 1 teaspoon organic olive oil

Directions:

1. Preheat the oven at 350 degrees F. Line a baking dish with parchment paper.
2. In a bowl, add all ingredients and toss to coat well.
3. Transfer the cashew mixture into a baking dish inside a single layer.
4. Roast for approximately 20 min, flipping once inside the middle way.
5. Remove from oven and make aside to cool before serving.
6. You can preserve these roasted cashews in an airtight jar.

Nutrition: Calories: 200, Fat: 17.13g, Carbohydrates: 10.65g, Fiber: 1.1g, Protein: 3.93g, Sodium: 100mg

75. ROASTED PUMPKIN SEEDS

Preparation time: 10 minutes

Cooking time: 20 minutes

Servings: 4

Ingredients:

- 1 cup pumpkin seeds, washed and dried
- 2 teaspoons garam masala
- 1/3 teaspoon red chili powder
- ¼ teaspoon ground turmeric
- Salt, to taste
- 3 tablespoons coconut oil, melted
- ½ tablespoon fresh lemon juice

Directions:

1. Preheat the oven at 350 degrees F.
2. In a bowl, add all ingredients except lemon juice and toss to coat well.
3. Transfer the almond mixture right into a baking sheet.
4. Roast approximately twenty or so minutes, flipping occasionally.
5. Remove from oven and make aside to cool before serving.
6. Drizzle with freshly squeezed lemon juice and serve.

Nutrition: Calories: 259, Fat: 24.71g, Carbohydrates: 4.72g, Fiber: 2g, Protein: 8.86g, Sodium: 82mg

76. SPICED POPCORN

Preparation time: 5 minutes

Cooking time: 2 minutes

Servings: 2-3

Ingredients:

- 3 tablespoons coconut oil
- ½ cup popping corn
- 1 tbsp olive oil
- 1 teaspoon ground turmeric
- ¼ teaspoon garlic
- Salt, to taste

Directions:

1. In a pan, melt coconut oil on medium-high heat.

2. Add popping corn and cover the pan tightly.

3. Cook, shaking the pan occasionally for around 1-2 minutes or till corn kernels begin to pop.

4. Remove from heat and transfer right into a large heatproof bowl.

5. Add essential olive oil and spices and mix well.

Nutrition: Calories: 261, Fat: 19.45g, Carbohydrates: 21.29g, Fiber: 2g, Protein: 2.3g, Sodium: 10mg

77. CUCUMBER BITES

Preparation time: 15 minutes

Cooking time: 0 minutes

Servings: 4

Ingredients:

- ½ cup prepared hummus
- 2 teaspoons nutritional yeast
- ¼-½ teaspoon ground turmeric
- Pinch of red pepper cayenne
- Pinch of salt
- 1 cucumber, cut diagonally into ¼-½-inch thick slices
- 1 teaspoon black sesame seeds
- Fresh mint leaves, for garnishing

Directions:

1. In a bowl, mix hummus, turmeric, cayenne, and salt.
2. Transfer the hummus mixture to the pastry bag and pipe on each cucumber slice.
3. Serve while using garnishing of sesame seeds and mint leaves.

Nutrition: Calories: 65, Fat: 3.09g, Carbohydrates: 7.1g, Fiber: 1.6g, Protein: 2.39g, Sodium: 164mg

78. SPINACH FRITTERS

Preparation time: 15 minutes

Cooking time: 5 minutes

Servings: 2-3

Ingredients:

- 2 cups chickpea flour
- ¾ teaspoons white sesame seeds
- ½ teaspoon garam masala powder
- ½ teaspoon red chili powder
- ¼ teaspoon ground cumin
- 2 pinches of baking soda
- Salt, to taste
- 1 cup water
- 12-14 fresh spinach leaves
- Olive oil, for frying

Directions:

1. In a sizable bowl, add all ingredients except spinach and oil and mix till an easy mixture form.
2. In a sizable skillet, heat oil on medium heat.
3. Dip each spinach leaf in chickpea flour mixture evenly and place in the hot oil in batches.
4. Cook, flipping occasionally for about 3-5 minutes or till golden brown from each side.
5. Transfer the fritters onto a paper towel-lined plate.

Nutrition: Calories: 244, Fat: 4.62g, Carbohydrates: 35.85g, Fiber: 6.9g, Protein: 3.96g, Sodium: 55mg

79. NO-BAKE STRAWBERRY CHEESECAKE

Preparation time: 20 minutes

Cooking time: 5 minutes

Servings: 8

Ingredients:

For Crust:

- 1 cup almonds
- 1 cup pecans
- 2 tablespoons unsweetened coconut flakes
- 6 Medjool dates, pitted, soaked for 10 min, and drained
- Pinch of salt

For Filling:

- 3 cups cashews, soaked and drained
- ¼ cup organic honey
- ¼ cup fresh lemon juice
- 1/3 cup coconut oil, melted
- 1 teaspoon organic vanilla flavor
- ¼ teaspoon salt
- 1 cup fresh strawberries, hulled and sliced

For Topping:

- 1/3 cup maple syrup
- 1/3 cup water
- 2 teaspoons vanilla extract
- 5 cups fresh strawberries, hulled, sliced, and divided

Directions:

1. Grease a 9-inch springform pan.
2. For crust in the small mixer, add almonds and pecans and pulse till finely ground.

3. Add remaining all ingredients and pulse till smooth.

4. Transfer the crust mixture into the prepared pan, pressing gently downwards. Freeze to create completely.

5. In a large blender, add all filling ingredients and pulse till creamy and smooth.

6. Place filling mixture over the crust evenly.

7. Freeze for at least a couple of hours or till set completely.

8. In a pan, add maple syrup, water, vanilla, and 1 cup of strawberries on medium-low heat.

9. Bring to a gentle simmer. Simmer for around 4-5 minutes or till thickens.

10. Strain the sauce and allow it to cool completely.

11. Top the chilled cheesecake with strawberry slices. Drizzle with sauce and serve.

Nutrition: Calories: 907, Fat: 69.63g, Carbohydrates: 71.33g, Fiber: 7.6g, Protein: 13.96g, Sodium: 364mg

80. RAW LIME, AVOCADO & COCONUT PIE

Preparation time: 20 minutes

Cooking time: 0 minutes

Servings: 8

Ingredients:

For Crust:

- ¾ cup unswee10ed coconut flakes
- 1 cup dates, pitted and chopped roughly

For Filing:

- ¾ cup young coconut meat
- 1½ avocados, peeled, pitted, and chopped
- 2 tablespoons fresh lime juice
- ¼ cup raw agave nectar

Directions:

1. Lightly, grease an 8-inch pie pan.
2. In a sizable food processor, add all crust ingredients and pulse till smooth.
3. Transfer the crust mixture into the prepared pan, pressing gently downwards.
4. With a paper towel, wipe out your blender completely.
5. In the same processor, add all filling ingredients and pulse till smooth.
6. Place filling mixture over the crust evenly.
7. Freeze not less than 120 minutes or till set completely.

Nutrition: Calories: 176, Fat: 10.34g, Carbohydrates: 22.6g, Fiber: 5.5g, Protein: 1.72g, Sodium: 27mg

81. PUDDING MUFFINS

Preparation time: 15 minutes

Cooking time: 26 minutes

Servings: 5

Ingredients:

For Muffins:

- 12 dates, pitted and chopped
- 10 tablespoons water
- 2½-3 tablespoons coconut flour
- ½ teaspoon baking powder
- 2 organic eggs
- 1½ bananas, peeled and sliced
- 1 teaspoon organic honey
- 1 tablespoon organic vanilla flavoring

For Topping:

- 5-6, pitted and chopped
- 3 tablespoons almond milk
- Fresh juice of ½ orange
- 1 teaspoon organic honey
- 1 teaspoon organic vanilla flavoring

For Garnishing:

- Fresh raspberries, as required

Directions:

1. Preheat the oven at 365 degrees F. Grease 5 cups of a large muffin tin.
2. For muffins in a tiny pan, mix dates and water on low heat.
3. Cook for approximately 3-4 minutes or till the dates break down and be thick.
4. Remove from heat and having a fork, mash the dates entirely.
5. In a bowl, add remaining ingredients and beat till well combined.
6. Add mashed dates and stir to combine.
7. Transfer the mix in prepared muffin cups evenly.
8. Bake for about 20-22 minutes.
9. Meanwhile, in a pan, add all topping ingredients on low heat.
10. Cook for about 3-4 minutes or till the dates break up and turn thick.
11. Remove from heat and having a fork mash the dates entirely. Keep aside.
12. Remove muffins from the oven and keep them aside to cool for approximately 5 minutes.
13. Carefully, take away the muffins from cups. Top with date mixture evenly.
14. Garnish with raspberries and serve

Nutrition: Calories: 477, Fat: 23.19g, Carbohydrates: 17.15g, Fiber: 1.5g, Protein: 48.37g, Sodium: 154mg

82. BLACK FOREST PUDDING

Preparation time: 15 minutes

Cooking time: 2 minutes

Servings: 2

Ingredients:

- 1 teaspoon coconut cream
- 1 teaspoon coconut oil
- 3-4 squares 70% chocolate bars, chopped
- 1 cup coconut cream, whipped till thick and divided
- 2 cups fresh cherries, pitted and quartered
- 70% chocolate bars shaving, for garnishing
- Shredded coconut, for garnishing

Directions:

1. In a smaller pan, add 1 teaspoon coconut cream, coconut oil, and chopped chocolate on low heat.
2. Cook, stirring continuously for about 2 minutes or till thick and glossy. Immediately, remove from heat.
3. In 2 glasses, divide chocolate sauce evenly.
4. Now, place ½ cup of cream over chocolate sauce in the glasses.
5. Divide cherries into glasses evenly.
6. Top with remaining coconut cream.
7. Garnish with chocolate shaving and shredded coconut.

Nutrition: Calories: 21670, Fat: 1552.15g, Carbohydrates: 1656.35g, Fiber: 391.8g, Protein: 282.44g, Sodium: 837mg

83. PINEAPPLE STICKS

Preparation time: 10 minutes

Cooking time: 0 minutes

Servings: 8

Ingredients:

- ¼ cup fresh orange juice
- ¾ cup coconut, shredded and toasted
- 8 (3x1-inch) new pineapple pieces

Directions:

1. Line a baking sheet with wax paper.
2. In a shallow dish, place pineapple juice.
3. In another shallow dish, squeeze pineapple.
4. Insert 1 wooden skewer in each pineapple piece through the narrow end.
5. Dip each pineapple piece in juice and then coat with coconut evenly.
6. Arrange the pineapple sticks onto a prepared baking sheet inside a single layer.
7. Cover and freeze for around 1-2 hours.

Nutrition: Calories: 65, Fat: 3g, Sat Fat: 3g Carbohydrates: 10g, Fiber: 1g, Protein: 0g Sodium: 25mg

84. FRIED PINEAPPLE SLICES

Preparation time: 15 minutes

Cooking time: 6 minutes

Servings: 6-8

Ingredients:

- 1 fresh pineapple, peeled and cut into large slices
- ¼ cup coconut oil
- ¼ cup coconut palm sugar
- ¼ teaspoon ground cinnamon

Directions:

1. Heat a large surefire skillet on medium heat.
2. Stir in oil and sugar till coconut oil is much melted.
3. Add pineapple slices in batches and cook for approximately 1-2 minutes.
4. Carefully flip the side and cook for around 1 minute.
5. Cook for approximately 1 minute more.
6. Repeat with remaining slices.
7. Sprinkle with cinnamon and serve.

Nutrition: Calories: 78, Fat: 3g, Sat Fat: 7.36g, Carbohydrates: 3.41g, Fiber: 0.2g, Protein: 0.2g, Sodium: 27mg

CONCLUSION

Antioxidants are a great way to rid the body of free radicals that cause inflammation and pain. These foods help with reducing inflammation, improving digestion, and protecting your cells from oxidative damage.

Most people easily see relief from these chronic conditions after just one day on this diet. If you are less than stimulated about following the whole elimination diet for 21 days, then feel free to add some of the previously forbidden foods back into your diet for variety and balance. Remember to continue avoiding inflammatory foods like gluten-containing grains, soybeans, peanuts, coffee beans, processed white sugar products like brownies or candy bars, as well as trans-fats containing margarine or shortening.

Some other tips that may help if you are interested in this diet:

1) Include some fresh vegetables every day. Try to avoid broccoli and cauliflower since they tend to spike your insulin level. Since the diet is the first place for inflammation to start, you should also be aware of the food you eat and its effects on the level of your body's inflammation. These foods have all been found to speed up signs of aging and might cause some damage in older people, so it is wise to steer clear of them.

2) Increase your water intake. The effect of water on the body is amazing and can help with many things. Drinking plenty of water is the best way to flush out toxins from your system and increase the circulation in your body.

3) Keep up with your weight. A healthy body needs to be well-proportioned and well-hydrated, so if you are a little overweight, drink more water to help you lose weight. However, diet is still key for good metabolism and improved energy levels that help with all health areas.

4) Try to avoid too much sugar in your diet. Sugar is best eaten in moderation and only on special occasions. Be aware of hidden sugar sources in foods like bread, ice cream, and yogurt so you can keep your daily sugar intake at a healthy level.

5) If you are sensitive to dairy products, look out for other dairy products that you might be able to eat without an upset stomach. Most lactose-intolerant people can tolerate yogurt and hard cheeses since they tend to have less lactose than milk.

If you have any ongoing health problems or medical issues such as chronic pain, gastrointestinal problems, or multiple sclerosis, you should always consult your physician before embarking on any new dietary plan. Those few simple steps will help you get the inflammation that is causing pain, aches, and symptoms under control.

Printed in Great Britain
by Amazon